The Way of Cats

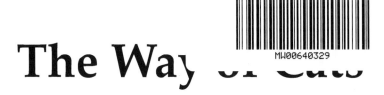

How to use their instincts to train, understand, and love them

by

Pamela Merritt

The Way of Cats
by
Pamela Merritt

Published by
WereBear Media, LLC
PO Box 131 Lake Placid, NY 12946

www.wayofcats.com

ISBN 978-0-9980357-0-3

For permissions contact:

writeme@WayofCats.com

Cover by Robert Merritt

Writing software by Literature and Latte
Scrivener & Scapple
(Simply the best!)

Dedicated to
Joseph Lenard Rothman
my first and greatest Cat Mentor

"By continually seeking to serve
the innocent and the good,
you stay in step with the Sage
and never wander alone in the world."

— Passage 56 of the *I Ching*

PAMELA MERRITT

CONTENTS

PAMELA MERRITT

The Cat on the Cover

It started with a name.

"Reverend Jim on *Taxi*," my husband said, referencing an old comedy show we both liked. "You know, he was goofy, mellow, sweet. I think that's the kind of cat we need."

I had brought two cats into the relationship with my husband. Now he was ready for us to raise one together. "So you can go out and find a kitten like that?"

"Sure," I said, having honed my kitten picking skills over years of cat rescue.

What I found was a four month old kitten who had been confiscated by the police. He was being held as a "material witness" in pending abuse charges. He had been starved nearly to death.

When our eyes met, he got up and came closer. I saw he was really a baby who had lost all of his baby fat.

I leaned towards his cage with only my head, keeping my hands behind my back so I wouldn't look threatening. "What's your story, Little Guy?"

He reached out his paws, claws tucked safely into his toes, and softly patted both my cheeks. He wanted love so much. *I can work with that*, I thought. *I know how to fix his other problems.*

But I couldn't bring him home yet, not until the shelter manager tracked down the arresting officer. I called the police station to make my case for release: this little guy had already bounced through three shelters who were trying to save him. It was Fading Puppy and Kitten Syndrome, and it could still kill him.

"His recovery is stalled because he needs a home," I told everyone I reached. "He needs focused attention. He is missing security, which he won't get in a cage with dogs barking and people constantly in and out. He needs to feel rescued."

I convinced them. The name turned out to fit him even more than anyone could have guessed.

Reverend Jim, the character in the classic situation comedy, had suffered a "time skip". He had fallen into the counter-culture in one decade, and only surfaced in another. So much had changed that everything he encountered was a surprise to him.

Reverend Jim, the kitten, had been severely neglected as well as starved. When I got him home, everything he encountered confused him.

The first thing my husband did was roll a toy towards him, and he only stared at it.

He didn't know how to play.

This was after three weeks of veterinary care. There is still fear in his eyes.

Why this Book

I created the Way of Cats to revolutionize any cat relationship.

I've been rescuing cats for decades. What I learned empowers me to say: no matter how good that cat relationship is now, *I can make it better*.

The Way of Cats simplifies care, creates training moments, and gives us the love we want by unlocking both our hearts.

I did not stop at rescue. I also rehabilitated. I have ways to help cats trust me, and tell me what they need, so they can heal.

Then I found cats their Forever Homes. By using my three Cat Types, I can teach the clues that will match a kitten or cat's personality to anyone's unique home.

Together, we can all learn the **Way of Cats**.

Communication

We reach cats through their brain.

Cats require a relationship based on friendship and equality.

We trade favors by understanding what each of us is trying to tell the other.

Reverend Jim was like someone with a Traumatic Brain Injury. Input overwhelmed him, and he would freeze.

For the longest time, he could only express himself through bursts of frantic activity. We could only guess at what he was asking for.

Once he began learning words like "hungry?" he had signals he could respond to. Knowing how to ask for what he needed soothed him. He began getting over the fear, and the panic.

Their Way

To care for, train, and love our cat, we must start with learning to read, and speak, Cat. I call this ability **Catspeak**.

Catspeak will let us manage our cat relationship smoothly, and with full cooperation.

• Communicate with our cat

• Figure out what they are asking for

• Give it to them

This solves training, care, and human affection. Because good communication is everything.

Yes, cats want Their Way. I grew to understand that they don't insist on things from stubbornness or stupidity or malice. Cats genuinely think their way is the best way.

I appreciate that. After all, I feel the same.

Cats have changed little from their wild ancestors. They are known as the least domesticated of all domesticated animals. So our cats remain beautifully adapted to their natural environment.

• The amazing thing is how easily they will adapt their wild instincts to our home environment. If we do things Their Way.

Cats are a unique pet

People are used to pets they either contain (like goldfish or canaries) or order around (like dogs and horses). The cat relationship is different, so different that **Cat Appreciators** cater to the cat's whims, and **Cat Skeptics** declare cats to be the worst pet ever.

But Cat Appreciators have it right, though often, they don't know exactly why. They only know that it works.

Turns out "catering to the cat's whims" is the right way to do things. We then enjoy a happy, loving, satisfying pet experience. It is also the only way that actually works. (I always prefer solutions which actually work.)

- It means we have to think of our cats, and ourselves, as mutually cooperative equals.

If we can't give the cat what they need, we will have a constant power struggle on our hands, where no one gets what they want, and everyone is unhappy. Neither of us will get cooperation and affection. The very point of having a cat, which is to enjoy an affectionate companion, will never happen.

- When we continually interfere with their survival instincts, the inevitable message we send is that we don't want them to live.

- They should not be treated as though they are under us. They do not think they are over us. They are friends on the same level.

When we do it right, cats are so easy, so rewarding, and so interactive. Cats become a secret people won't believe when we first tell them.

Using psychology

Cats are not compelled to be affectionate, as pack animals are. Cats only reciprocate with affection when they are treated with affection.

- Trading favors is so important to proper cat management I call it the **Law of Reciprocity.**

I didn't make up this law. Human psychology did. When referring to humans, it means we do favors for people who do favors for us. When referring to cats, it means the same thing. Cats understand favor-giving, and they are absolutely compelled to return a sweet gesture. It is practical magic which works on all kinds of cats.

Cats are not frustrating and mysterious when we act on this simple law. Cats will leave our stuff alone, be happy to see us, and show affection freely; once we start doing them favors. They cannot help it.

• Cats have a finely tuned sense of social obligations and an amazing ability to discern fairness.

All they need is a secure foundation and an environment which meets their needs. Creating a relaxed cat creates a trusting, happy, and affectionate cat.

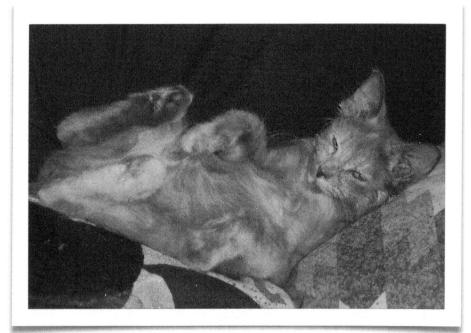

Olwyn relaxing comfortably in her new home.

Once we have a communication line established with our cat or kitten, we can help them meet their needs in ways which please both of us.

• They won't misbehave because we will be able to show them how we would like them to to behave.

The best part? We do it all with *games*.

Learn the games, play forever

Fun Games are the way we do training and communication and love. I have many **Affection Moves** which let us say "I love you" in Catspeak.

This will make our cats so happy they will seek us out for more games. Have productive discussions, negotiate terms, and experience heart-melting moments.

As a science fiction fan, I longed to explore new worlds and meet beings from another planet. Cats are the next best thing. A great cat relationship is psychology and perspective and insight. We might approach our goals in ways that don't seem to intersect, until we realize we have mutual interests after all.

There's humor and compassion and that moment we connect with a loving spark that leaps between our two species.

• Am I making cats sound like the most fun ever?

• That is because: *they are.*

When Punishment Fails

Bond, James Bond. He was a feral kitten, and saved from the kill shelter when I showed him he could bond with me. But then... he didn't want to bond with anyone else, and I had to bring him home.

"Cat training" is considered a contradiction in terms. This creates two approaches when it comes to cats as pets.

• There are the people who claim cats are *untrainable* and praise dogs for this quality.

• There are the people who love cats enough to shrug and *let them have their way.*

• Both of these approaches have *drawbacks.*

In the first instance, people scorn cats for what they see as a lack of intelligence. This leads to other disparagements, such as the view of cats as manipulative con artists who don't really care about affection. (Even though that would take intelligence...)

In the second, while things are far better in the affection category, people find themselves unable to help when the cat does need some guidance. Our domestic cats live in our world, not their natural one, and could use some help figuring things out.

When the student is ready, the teacher appears

I lost my first husband to a sudden illness, which collapsed much of everything, including my long-time, amateur, cat rescue operation. After getting new homes for everyone else, I wound up with the two shyest, hard-to-place cats, James Bond and Smokepuff.

I was able to build a new life with the person my blog readers know as Mr WayofCats. When we both decided to take Cultural Anthropology in college, he didn't know our developing relationship would lead to him taking Cat Anthropology from me. He'd grown up with cats and welcomed the three of us.

He was also my first student in learning the Way of Cats. "I thought I knew cats," he once told me, with wonder. "This experience is several levels up from anything I knew was possible." We now live with our four rescue cats; Reverend Jim, Princess Olwyn, Sir Tristan, and Mithrandir the Magician.

I had showed him that, for cats, everything is about friendship. They will respond to our invitation to *do favors for each other*. Which is my favorite way of getting things done.

This is not the Marines

People think "training" is when we tell the being what to do and they do it.

Because if they don't do it, we will make things unpleasant for them. Many people try "negative discipline" where they punish the cat for doing something wrong.

The thought process is like this:

• When the cat does something we don't like, we do something the cat doesn't like.

• Then the cat will realize we don't want them to do that, because when they do, something bad happens.

• Right? Wrong. So very wrong. (There's your problem.)

We assume the cat will think their actions triggered the Bad Thing that happened. But cats are too smart for that; they know *we* did the Bad Thing to *them*. So they sensibly decide that the element they should be avoiding here is *us*.

Cats respond to punishment by getting upset, which keeps them from thinking, because their first response to danger is to *escape it as fast as possible*. If they cannot do that, they panic.

Being insistent on "punishing" our cats for misbehavior only teaches our cats that we are untrustworthy and should be avoided. Then they will misbehave even more, because they are still miserable *and* getting no guidance *and* still doing that thing we don't like.

• It is one of the most difficult things in the world to admit we are *creating our own problems*.

• It is one of the most joyous things in the world to realize *we can stop doing that.*

People think they only have two choices: *punish* the cat or *ignore* a problem behavior. Instead we can play a Fun Game to let the cat know there's a better way to do what they want to do. We then encourage them to perform this suggested, better, behavior instead, and praise them happily when they do.

We can communicate with cats. It is easy and enjoyable and increases our happiness and then we get more love.

Win-win

It takes a certain amount of self-awareness and confidence for us to *simply be lovable,* trust our cat to notice, and respond to our requests because they love us.

But it can be done.

A spectacular way punishment backfires is that the cat stops doing the thing… in front of us. But we find little footprints on the kitchen counter and feel upset and angry. Now we try to catch them at it so we can punish them. They avoid us more.

By putting the cat in a panicked state, we force the cat to focus on the obnoxious things *we are doing,* not the obnoxious thing our *cat is doing.* They will sensibly switch to doing that thing (that thing their instincts insist they do) when we are not around. Since so much misbehavior is stress-related, they will probably do it even more than before.

Since cats communicate amongst themselves with **Body Language**, they *show* us what they need by *doing* what they need. We might not like the behavior, but we cannot help the cat choose a better behavior by becoming angry.

When we have mutual respect and affection operating in the relationship, the only barrier to each of us getting what we want is sharing our wants and needs with each other.

• Cat *wants* are cat *needs.*

Then we can happily do each other favors, which also increases the exchange of affection and gives more power to our requests. We need to look at our cat's misbehavior as a signal to us that we should provide them with better ways of doing whatever it is.

Because whatever the cat is doing, it is a behavior that their instincts tell them they absolutely *have to do*. We can help them find a way of doing it that we won't mind.

Remove the idea of punishment when it comes to our cat relationships. Actually, it wouldn't hurt to remove the idea of punishment from most of what we do. The only thing cruelty does is add to the total amount of cruelty in the world.

No good will come of that.

Positive Discipline

Cats don't think of *anything* they do as bad. As humans, we have a counterproductive tendency to paste this label on anything our cats do that we don't like. While our cats see their behavior, always, as a means of meeting their important needs.

• The answer to "Can I *make* the cat do this thing?" is always "No."

• What we can do is *make* the cat *want* something.

Communication is our greatest tool.

• We have to be able to tell the cat that we don't want them to do that.

• *because:*

• It is the only way they are ever going to know we want them to stop doing that

Some of our Fun Games will use **Positive Discipline** to focus on convincing our cats that they should welcome our input. If we become a trusted source of information, they will listen to our advice about their behavior. All good friends want to know the house rules.

Cooperation works both ways. If we have the litter box or food dish in a bad place, our cat will try to convey that information to us. It may *look* like misbehavior, but if we reflexively, and constantly, treat it as such, we will only frustrate both of us.

A cat's instincts compel them to find a way to have their needs met. Demonstrating the inadequacy of the present setup might be the only way they know to get that point across.

Redirection

What I call **Redirection** is the best response to misbehavior. This lets us handle a cat who keeps going after something they shouldn't, by giving them something they can have.

• Energy cannot be extinguished, only *redirected*.

Cats always want to have their needs met, but if we show them that our way is better, they will happily do the new thing. They will even feel grateful to us for giving them an upgrade in their care.

Positive Discipline is guidance that teaches. If punishment is often the first thing we think of, we must retrain ourselves with the realization that it is not that great a teaching tool. It actually makes little sense even for their own good; we don't want the cat to get hurt on a hot stove, so we hurt the cat? That's a disconnect in logic that anyone would have trouble following.

Cats off the counters: the way that works

The real solution to keeping the cat off the kitchen counters is to *give the cat what they want*.

Put out a kitchen stool, designate the top of the fridge, or offer the upper surface of a cabinet that will let them get up there without stepping on things they should not. Put pieces of cat furniture near their routes so they can scratch something that signals ownership, as their survival instincts urge them to do.

In nature, cats have various spots to do the important work of monitoring all activity in their hunting territory. This instinctual need does not go away when they live with us.

We need to get over thinking that the cat can watch from the floor. Why won't they do that? Because they can't really see from the floor, and they are also underfoot on the floor, and we don't want them milling around on the floor when we are trying to prepare food. Such an approach makes them feel vulnerable and frightened and us feel exasperated and annoyed.

We do both of us a favor if we create and gift them:

This play tunnel makes our recovering feral, Mithrandir, feel secure. It moves from room to room.

- their own **Outpost**, a place where they can hang out and be with us
- introduce it with happy voices to let our cat know it's a gift

• **Bless the Spot** by placing them in it to signal our approval

Put them on it whenever they are making a nuisance of themselves in the kitchen. We can point to it and tell them to go there. A few repeats and they will understand the wonderful gift we have given them.

• They get to stay in their Outpost when they stay in their Outpost.

Now, we are both happy.

• Isn't this… *giving in* to the cat? Sure.

• Doesn't this make the cat… our *Boss*? Yes.

• Our cat *knows better than we do* when it comes to what they need.

Once we have gifted them their kitchen Outpost, we can simply move them from the counter to their Outpost and be happy and pleased they have a spot to be in without getting into trouble.

Explain why we gave them this Outpost — it was for their own safety. Because the next time we see our cat on the counter, we should act shocked — *shocked* — that they are on the counter.

• Project *worry*, not *anger*.

Tell them this isn't a good place for them, and use a cleaning spray on that area with great gusto, and clean it off. This takes care of our cleanliness issues, and it also lets our cat know we are looking out for them. *That area was about to be sprayed. It could happen again at any moment.*

• Is it *ever* too late?

• No, we can always do what we should have done in the first place.

• It is easier to *train us to do it right* than argue with the cat.

Why can't the cat stay out of the kitchen? They have a strong interest in where the food happens. Why can't the cat leave the kitchen when we want them to? Because they have such a strong interest in being with their people and sharing their lives.

We got the cat for companionship. We are getting it.

World They Did Not Make

The ways our cats cope with our world might seem strange to us. Until we realize it is, after all, *not their world*; not the world their instincts have equipped them to survive in. They do live in a **World They Did Not Make**.

I am continually amazed that cats are such successful and enjoyable pets, because very little in our domestic world matches a desert environment teeming with vermin.

A good thing, too. Neither of us are living there now.

• We humans are often puzzled by our cat's behaviors.

• Our cat always has a good reason for what they do.

• We simply need to find out what that reason is.

They use their wild instincts to get what they need from the human world. Sometimes it works well, and sometimes it doesn't, but it wouldn't be fair to get mad at them for things they cannot help doing.

Cat Territory Thinking

"Why does my cat climb the drapes and claw the couch? Why am I always chasing them off the bookcase and the refrigerator? Why can't cats leave things alone?"

They can't, that's why.

A cat's instinctive response to danger is to climb something and get above it. Their hunting skills require them to scope out their territory, and they like high vantage points to survey as much as possible. They need Outposts in every room we spend time in, because they want to spend time with us. We should be flattered, not annoyed.

• Cats are terraformers; used to adjusting their own territory to suit them.

They put their whole body into scratching because it's more than claw sharpening; it's a territory signal, stress-relieving exercise, and a show of happiness and satisfaction. Couches and chairs are attractive to them because flimsy won't cut it.

When cats are disruptive about their scratching behaviors, it's the behavior of an animal who needs trees... and doesn't have any. Solve it by giving them some scratching posts with the qualities they are looking for.

Mixed signals

"Why do they scratch and bite? Why can't they play nice? Why don't they want to sit on my lap and cuddle?"

This is simply the cat's response to the wrong ways people try to connect with them. Bouncing our hand on their heads, grabbing for their belly, and using our hand as a toy; these are all ways we send the wrong signal to our cats.

We are trying to say *I'm a friend*, but what our body language says is, *Let's play rough*. So, cats do, especially if we try to make them respond to us the way we want.

I often hear complaints that a cat lured them in for petting and then attacked, but this always turns out to be a story about a human who doesn't understand clear cat signals of annoyance like folded back ears, a lashing tail, and making a noise like an air raid siren.

• Wanting to pet a cat doesn't mean we should.

Their hunting instincts are not the only instincts we are working with. Cats have social instincts, too. In their original state they lived in colonies, where kitten care and food gathering were shared activities. They have ways of showing affection, and if we use those ways, our message will get through.

If we are having trouble getting our cat to understand something, it never hurts to let them know we want them to be happy and safe. Hurt feelings on either side will only get in the way of our efforts to please each other, so we should try to give our cats the benefit of the doubt. The more loving our relationship, the more the cat will give us points for effort.

Tristan expending some energy in his favorite spot, on his cat tree, with one of his herbal toys.

Cats will live happily in our world because they love us. They do their best to provide the companionship, interaction, and enjoyment that is their part of the pet deal.

They trust us to take care of the parts they can't manage themselves.

Translation, Please

Encourage the cat to talk to us by talking to them, using a Fun Game I call **Subtitling**.

• Combine our human words with expressive body language

• Make our voices full of emotion

• Use facial expressions and gestures for dramatic emphasis

Our cats can't pass a vocabulary test, but we will be surprised at how much they can grasp when we make the effort to Subtitle ourselves:

• when we express affection

• suggest a better way of getting what they want

• explain that the store was out of their favorite flavor

Be expressive with our cat
They can more easily figure out the message if it is coming from three sources: our voice, our facial expression, and our body postures. This is how they "talk" between themselves.

So our voice, our face, and our hands are the way we signal *how we feel*.

• If our cat is *misbehaving*, we are sad.

• If our cat is *showing* us something, we are curious.

• If our cat is *giving* us attention, we are affectionate.

Cats who stare intently into our face are saying they want the object of their gaze to do something; find the toy, acknowledge them, start dinner. Any happy attention we direct at our cat is always welcome. If we show that we want to listen to them, they will tell us more things.

When my cats twirl in front of me, or stare intently until I get up, I know they want me to ask questions and follow them around. Sometimes they want me to do something. Sometimes they want us to enjoy some time together.

If our cat is trying to catch our attention, *give them some*. This is how a relationship gets built.

- Use our emotion to connect with their emotions.

Let them know we love them by using our voice and face to express how we feel. Speaking in soft tones, using their name in a silly song, or giving them a slow blink as we pass each other in the hall; all of this lets them know we are thinking of them.

Cat Kisses are one of the most powerful of all Cat Affection Moves. This is the equivalent of a human smile, and we give it by looking into a cat's eyes and blinking, with a little squint to our eyes as they become fully closed. A few gentle, slow-motion, blinks and the cat might be compelled to cat-smile back with a few Cat Kisses of their own.

We can **Pet With Our Voice**. Cats have hearing that is much more sensitive than our own. So the closer we get, the softer we should speak. If our head is close to their head, we should barely be speaking at all. This works for us; we get much more emotion in our voice when we remember our **Volume Control**.

- Our cats have super-senses that can easily be overloaded with too much input.

If we have ever noticed our cat "bothers" us when we are talking on the phone, it can be puzzling. We start an enjoyable human conversation, and suddenly our cat will appear, wanting something.

People assume the worst, such as jealousy, or that they are being deliberately interrupted by the cat wanting to be fed or played with.

Olwyn demonstrates a Cat Kiss, the blink of the eyes which is a cat smile.

How can our cat realize we are talking to another, invisible, person? This is not a concept that is easy for a cat to understand. So when we walk around talking, they think *it's about them.*

We're excited and animated, and our cat *loves* that. So cope with it by petting them and making eye contact and letting them feel that all this thrilling voice stuff is about *them.*

Too much input

Cats don't like loud voices or big gestures. We may be excited, but they see this as threatening. Consider sights and sounds, and also our waving arms and running footsteps, as part of their input. Too much input needs Volume Control.

• We need to move slowly and talk softly when we are trying to communicate.

Since their senses are more powerful than our own, they are taking in a lot more information than we can, making them more easily overwhelmed by too much input.

Even the pleasurable acts of grooming, petting, and playing with our cats can *become too stimulating*. For the cat to handle the vast input they get from our interactions, the cat needs to rely on our trust and love, so they know how to handle the feelings we are creating.

When a cat starts lashing their tail and biting at the comb or toy we are using, it's a sign for us to back off and let them process the stimulus they already have, not add more. Many people don't realize how they are sending wrong messages to the cat during play. When we become aggressive with our body language, we are pushing the cat into responding in kind.

Our cat mirrors the way we treat them. If we are gentle and affectionate, they will be too.

Mimes

How do our cats convey their requests? They use their Body Language.

• Cats are **Mimes**.

Knowing that helps us understand how cats, lacking human language, will "act out" their intentions.

Our cats will rub their faces or their shoulders on something when they want to claim it as something they "own" or enjoy. If they do this to us, they are declaring *You are mine*. Pet them to agree. If we see them happy with their new cat tree, we can respond verbally: "What a good kitty, using your new scratcher."

Reverend Jim is an amazing case study in how cats learn to express themselves and ask for things. As in humans, a kitten who lacks a rich environment for experimentation and play can develop a mind which struggles with symbolic concepts.

We might not realize it, but cats use abstract thinking all the time. They know those mice are fake. They know the grocery bag might contain treats, even if they can't see the treats. They know the suitcase means we might be going away, even though they don't know where or why.

We taught Reverend Jim how to play, the ways the other cats liked to be treated, and what we did to let him know to leave certain things alone. Always, we worked on his words. He learned his name, his nicknames, "breakfast", "dinner", "hungry", "James Bond", and "Smokepuff".

One day I had refreshed the cats' water bowl, and noticed he was sitting expectantly on the kitchen floor. He was giving me an intent stare.

I said, "I put new water in the bowl," as so many times before. He looked over at the water bowl. *He had learned a new word.*

Another morning, Reverend Jim appeared for breakfast. Too early, as usual. I rolled over and ignored him. When he came back at the right time, I greeted him with, "Do you want something?"

Reverend Jim was slow at first, but he would get there. He would use Mime to let us know what he was thinking.

I was ready to follow up more specifically, but this time Reverend Jim reared back and stared down at the floor. This is how I know when he is thinking. He has to work through it. He knew I was telling him something, but he didn't know what.

But before I could speak again, his face transformed, as though the sun had come up in his mind. He bounced over, all excited. *Yes. He wanted something.*

"Something" had dawned on him. He had mastered the abstract noun.

That was the moment he made the connection between "something" and the concept of *something he wants*. Now his development accelerated, as his brain had reached a new level in ability.

Ask them to tell us

How can a cat convey what they want? We play **Show Me**.

• When a cat wants my attention, I get up.

• I move a little in whatever direction they are going.

• I happily say, "Show Me."

• I follow them around and if they seem interested in something, I touch it.

• If this gets them excited, I am on the right track.

• Repeat.

It's like the game of "Hot and Cold" children play. When we are on the wrong track, our cat tries to correct us. If we are on the right one, our cat gets more excited. This is how they lead me to the object of their interest. This is how I get them what they ask for.

I have found that expressing my emotions with exaggerated body language and expressive voice tones will let even young kittens know what I am feeling.

• By being *visibly worried* when they play with something they shouldn't, I am saying that I am keeping them away from it because of *fears for their safety*. (Which often has the benefit of being true.)

• My *sadness* when they forget their manners is a subtle, and non-threatening, reminder of our agreement to make each other happy.

• My *happiness* when they cooperate or act affectionate feeds their happiness, and we increase the total amount of love in the world.

This is why we should always *apologize* if we frighten or disappoint them. Because without us trying to reassure them, they will be puzzled and cautious. If we drop a pan while they were in the kitchen and scared them, let them know it was an accident and you didn't mean to.

• Unless we *sound* sorry, they won't know we are sorry.

Likewise, if the cat does something we like, let them know. If we tell them when they make us happy, they will try to make us happy more often. Sharing these good feelings of happiness is why we are having a cat relationship.

Emotions have great power. Let's use them for good.

Cat Radio

Cats talk to us all the time. Do we listen?

When we understand what our cat is saying with their Body Language, we are able to pick up their signals.

• I call this tuning the **Cat Radio.**

• Until we "turn on the radio" we won't get the signal.

Too often, a person who feels summoned will get up, check the food and litter, find it okay, and then ignore the cat. But that is not the only tune coming through the radio. Our cat wants more from the relationship than simply having their physical needs met.

At one point in his kittenhood, Reverend Jim was not his usual excited self at mealtime. When he did not follow his dish into the bathroom, I puzzled over what this behavior was trying to tell me. I realized he was saying he disliked his incarceration there, which started because he wouldn't leave the other cats' food alone.

If I hadn't been "tuned" to his highly physical ways of communicating, I would not have picked up this signal that he didn't want to eat in the bathroom any more. He had decided to behave himself with the other cats during dinner. He let me know this by sitting in the middle of the kitchen floor, where polite cats waited for their bowl.

The only way he could tell me he didn't want to eat in the bathroom was to not eat in the bathroom.

So, I gave him a chance, telling him he has to act like a big boy, which meant no stealing the other cats' food. He understood, and showed off the manners he had learned. This also signaled a breakthrough in his communication abilities, which were too often expressed by him racing around like a bottle rocket.

Giant Sensory Map

Cats have super-senses that let them monitor more of their territory than we can. This leads to them living in the middle of what I call the **Giant Sensory Map**.

Their hearing is more acute in both the low and the high registers. Their vision is not as sharp in details as a human's, but is far better than ours at detecting motion. This affinity for movement helps them understand both their native language and our attempts at Catspeak.

Their highly developed senses lets them build a three dimensional map of their territory. They keep track of every possible change that occurs in it.

- When they aren't patrolling it with their bodies, they are "patrolling" it with their keen senses.

Understanding our cat's Giant Sensory Map, which can vary from cat to cat, is key to figuring out many processes in their lives. We can reap the benefits of being part of their Map. They can pick up what we are broadcasting on our own radio.

Cats can have varying ideas of what encompasses their territory, and how much authority they can exercise in it, but they all monitor boundaries. Something new is always noticed, because it *might be prey*, or it might be something that thinks *they are prey*. Either way, they need to know.

- Their response to events is based on how something makes them *feel*.
- To communicate with us, they will try to show how they *feel*.

My cat Smokepuff would ask for treats by pretending he barely had the strength to drag himself across the rug at my feet. Then he would raise one trembling paw, to emphasize that this was a desperate appeal for goodies.

I knew it was an act, but admired the depth of feeling he could put into a simple request for treats.

This is an example of how cats can exaggerate a feeling they already have, making it bigger so humans can understand it.

Smokepuff got confused when humans wore hats, but he was a brilliant dramatist.

If, as often happened, he'd recently had a treat, I would tell him so. He would spring up and go find his pillow to sleep on. He knew there was no harm in asking. Especially when I was so charmed by the way he asked.

If I didn't pay attention to Smokepuff, I would miss his little play, which we called The Trembling Paw. I would hurt his feelings. We wouldn't have these Fun Games together.

Turn on the Cat Radio. Hear what comes through.

Cat Database

To make decisions about how to react to things, cats draw upon what I call the **Cat Database**. This is the cat's memory, which science thinks is very good, roughly the same as a six-year-old human's. The way cats use their warehouse of memories reminds me of a how a database keeps track of all the boxes of things in a warehouse.

How large is the cat's database? Virtually limitless. It stores everything that has ever happened to the cat since before they opened their eyes. All these memories are boxes in a warehouse.

A database is a way of storing information in a computer, like the way every box in the warehouse has a description attached to it. The database keeps track so stuff won't get lost in the warehouse.

Think of the aisles as behaviors cats perform every day. When a cat *scratches their scratching post* is one aisle. When a cat comes at the *sound of the can opener* is another aisle.

When the cat's mind zips its forklift down the aisle where these memories are stored, they will instantly know what to think of *what had happened*:

- One side of the aisle is everything *good*.

- The other side of the aisle is everything *bad*.

- The *bigger* the box, the more good or bad it was.

So when the cat goes mentally looking for can opener sound, there should be many lovely big boxes. There's a few on the bad side of the aisle, but they are small, the times the cat came for green beans and went away disappointed.

That's why the cat always comes at the sound of the can opener. Because it's not terrible if it's not for them, and so good when it is for them.

Don't clutter the aisles

It's another reason why we can't train with punishment. The bad things are in such big boxes the cat forklift can't even get down the aisle. That does not leave much room for us to wedge in good events to make up for it. Better to not clutter up that aisle in the first place.

- Everything we do puts a box in the cat's mental warehouse, a record in the Cat Database.

We pluck kittens off the couch, transfer them to their cat tree, and act happy when they climb it. We are training them in ways appropriate to their developmental stage.

By "teleporting" them to the right thing, they learn to seek out the cat tree when they want to climb. We are building a set of environmental cues that will work without us being there, and without scaring the kitten or making them fear us.

Because we have used Catspeak to tell the kitten to move from the couch to the scratching post — by actually moving them from the couch to the scratching post — we are building a sequence of events in our kitten's Cat Database.

- We delivered a box.

- We made the box bigger.

- It's a happy box.

As our kitten's mind matures, we can make the mental image of a thing appear in their minds with our words. When I tell my cats "dinner", they know I mean "food for them as dusk approaches". Back at the warehouse, "food" has lots of giant happy boxes. They will come when I say "dinner", since "dinner" is a summons for a particular thing they like.

Of course the cat knows their name. They know all their nicknames, too. They don't come at all to the sound of their name if we don't use it properly. This is how the cat has developed an incorrect reputation for not even knowing their name.

Our cats do think about things. Especially Mithrandir, who is learning how to live with humans.

• Cats will come when their names are called — when we call them only for good things.

Once a memory box has appeared in the Cat Database, such as I came when I heard my name called and they crammed this pill down my throat, this is the box that will block the aisle.

It takes many, many entries like *I came when I heard my name called and got a fishy treat* to make up for it. We will have to *call* their name and *bring* them the fishy treat quite a few times before we grow the happy-box big enough to make the unhappy-box shrink by comparison.

Suppose we call the cat, and they come. If we only say "hello" and not follow up with anything notable for them, we have created an entry in the database. The cat didn't mind, but it is not going to build a strong drive to *come when my name is called*.

If we are happy to see them, we can get them onto our lap, ask them to hang around us when we are doing things, and show them a thing they might be curious about. Getting them to enjoy coming to their name will only happen when we supply instant and positive feedback.

• Cats are thrilled when we show that we are thrilled by them.

The proper way to be upset if the cat misbehaves is to be *sad*. Act upset over the tipped-over lamp, distressed over the scattered stack of papers from our desk, and miserable over the broken decoration. This will convey the proper emotional mood, so our cat will be able to connect their action with our distress.

Our actions towards the cat are extremely powerful in shaping their behavior, which is all based on their meticulous information system. When we fill their Cat Database with respect and consideration, we will get happy cats who want to please us.

Cat Etiquette

Cats have their own etiquette rules. By knowing and using **Cat Etiquette**, our friendship gestures will be seen as they are meant. We were not born to the cat's world, but a few central guidelines makes their rules easy to follow.

• It never hurts to be *respectful* of their person.

Part of showing respect is being aware of the big size difference between ourselves, and our cat.

Imagine we're getting ready to leave for the day, and want our cat to know we are going to miss them. It can seem thoughtful to seek them out, pick them up, and carry them around with us while we grab our stuff and put the lid on the coffee. Then we leave them by the front door.

While our cat appreciates the hugging and sweet words, we haven't been all that considerate. How would we feel if our favorite giant showed up to drag us out of bed and lugged us around while hugging us? Would we feel loved about being left on the floor?

If we had sought our napping cat out, to pet them without moving them, we will be conveying our love without mixing our message.

Petting in Place

Yanking our cat from their relaxation tells our cat we don't understand how relaxed they were. That posture a cat assumes is not as easy as it looks; they have carefully arranged all their pieces for maximum rest.

When they are in such a position, it is much more loving to simply express our love, by **Petting in Place**, without rearranging them in the process.

Tristan is our most "boneless" cat.

• To love cats, we should love *subtlety*. As they do.

We want to hug them; they want to continue relaxing in the pose they have chosen. So we do both, by leaving them where they are, and moving our body instead. Because this is the only move that will make us both happy.

Our cats are about *one tenth* of our own size, or less. To be suddenly yanked away from whatever they are doing, and being dumped somewhere else, is considered… rude.

Reminding ourselves that we are giant creatures to our cats is a useful mindset for any cat interaction.

Flirt with the cat

If we have ever noticed the way people who don't like cats seem to draw them like a magnet, we now know how to draw cats to us like a magnet.

The more the cat-shy try to signal they don't like cats, the more the cats misunderstand their intentions. Because, to the cats, it such behavior looks like it is *beckoning them closer*.

By doing what they do, we can perform the magic we want. We can draw the cat to us.

—*Be coy*. If we are paying constant attention to where the cat is, what they are doing, shyly avoiding their eyes, and turning away when the cat studies us; this is saying, *I'm not going to watch you, so you can watch me in comfort*.

—*Use Cat Kisses*. Those who fear cats become very still when the cat is near, and often blink nervously. The nervous blinking looks like the slow blinks of cat friendship.

—*Be still*. Fearful people freeze up, but this looks like it is inviting calm investigation, the way a cat likes it. This is exactly what other cats do to convey friendliness and invite an approach.

—*Let cats pet themselves with us*. The fearful make "warding off" gestures, holding out a downward-curved hand, afraid to make sudden movements. To the cat, this looks like they are willing to extend a *passive hand*, which invites the cat to pet themselves with it at the speed they like.

• When a person who is **Cat Fearful** make themselves a passive object willing to be investigated, they don't realize they are constantly signaling *Please become fascinated with me, as I am with you*.

In Catspeak, they are telling the cat that they should explore this fascinating person who seems to know all the right cat things to say.

Cat Imagination

In the beginning, there isn't much thought.

Kittens automatically chase things that move, much as babies automatically put things in their mouths. It's how they experience the world.

While one of the delights of kitten raising is watching them grow from baffled bundles of bouncy joy into thoughtful thinkers and planners, this development does not stop throughout the cat's lifetime. Cats continually learn new things and grow in mental power.

Even though they are eating out of cans, they still need to exercise their hunting instincts:

- observe the prey

- anticipate the prey

- ambush the prey

Make a point of setting aside time to play with our cat. If our cat is left to amuse themselves, *they will*.

We are better off providing toys, creating reliable play times, and coming up with new Fun Games.

Everything can be a game

Throwing a sponge ball or waving a wand toy isn't only for getting our cat needed exercise or make them stop bothering us. These games re-create part of the cat's natural environment for them. They use their imagination to turn the toy into prey.

But we can also play training, care, and affection games. Show Me is practical, because it lets us agree to a cat request. It's also fun, as a game where we guess at what our cat is showing us.

They even make up their own games. Tristan trots to the door when he wants it opened for him, to play on our enclosed stairwell. But if I stop midway, so does he.

In his mind, he isn't running to the door and waiting for me to open it. He is escorting me to the door, so we can have our chat about what he wants to do, and I can remind him to "Be careful out there."

While he is pressing buttons on his human to get what he wants, that's not all he wants. Part of the fun of getting me to open and close the door for him are these discussions and rituals, where I show interest in what interests him.

Cat Toys

Cat toys get reviews with the complaint, "But my cat got bored with it." Cats get bored with any toy. **Toy Rotation** is the secret to happy cat amusement.

Cats are intelligent creatures. So they need new toys, they need new ways to play with the old toys, and they need some level of freedom to play with their toys the way they need to.

Consider our cat's favorite toy modes:

—*Bat around and chase toys.* Toy mice, crinkly balls, springy shapes, and the balls with bells in them. "Hockey cats" are looking for lots of action, and room to really get going.

—*Ninja cats enjoy the hunt.* They like to stalk, chase, and ambush their prey. They love wand toys like the Bird Catcher PRO, Cat Dancer, da Bird, fishing pole arrangements with a toy on the end, or even a length of yarn with a ball of paper tied to it. (Be careful of fine string, or plastic strips.)

—*Wand toys require a person.* They shouldn't be left out. The cat will not be able to resist attacking when its back is turned, but they might get tangled in it or ruin the toy. They are wonderful for play sessions when we want the cat to expend a lot of energy, such as before bed.

—*Study cats* want to see changes happen, with or without their input. Sealed water toys or a toy left floating in the half filled bathroom sink are good for these cats, as are crackly toys.

—*Cat videos* are especially popular with window watchers, but most cats will enjoy fish in a tank or birds at a feeder. There are Youtube channels produced for their special interests; they don't mind the commercials that much.

Tristan on his cat tree. Pondering his favorite activity.

Try out the different kinds of toys, and keep some in a basket the cat has access to. Put away others, so they can sit in storage and spark new interest when they come out. Some cats will swap their own toys in and out of their toy box. Other cats will be interested in a new toy the second or third time it comes around, because they will have had time to ponder it.

Catnip toys, in which the greatest attraction was the catnip, grow stale fast. They can be recharged with the right herbs, like our *Way of Cats* Herbal Cat Products. We can put the toys in a bag and bread them like chicken pieces. This will activate the scented oils that is the source of their appeal.

Some toys will get broken and we should get rid of them. However, if the cat seeks that toy, we should get more like it, so our cat can have their favorite back.

Toys are also a powerful way of luring cats away from things they shouldn't play with. If we are trying to convince our cat to "leave that alone" we should study the object for clues. This can be valuable information about what attracts them. We can use this to make better toy choices.

Cause and Effect

We must remember that cats are scientists. They not only understand **Cause and Effect**, they will actively pursue *causes* to get desired *effects*.

By learning what happens when they do something, and what they can do to make that thing happen again, cats continually seek to repeat happy events.

Key to training

Even young kittens do this with their constant exploration. The more we can create a routine for them, the faster they will figure out what comes first, and what comes next.

• play or grooming session

• then a treat session

• end with cuddling

They will soon start putting these happy events together. This is how they learn *when* they can expect these events, and *what* they are supposed to do during them.

What kittens have working against them are their teeny-tiny attention spans. But this also means they are easily distracted. *Gently distracting them when they are misbehaving* is a very solid technique. Soon they will avoid the trouble areas all by themselves. At this tiny age, we move in small steps, happily repeating our instructions and moving them to their scratching post, their toy area, or their cat tree as needed.

This helps with teen rule setting, since they love to test boundaries, much like human teens. But why? Aren't we telling them the same things we have been saying since they were tiny? Well, yes. But they have changed.

As our cat's mind embarks upon maturation, their increased intellectual prowess allows them to start testing everything. Including our patience and our love. The best thing we can do for our teen cat is remind them that we love them. Even when they seem to be ignoring us.

Because they are, in Catspeak, asking for a deeper, more adult, relationship. Ironically, the mere fact that they have learned so much about how we want them to behave means we are actually paying less attention to them lately.

A closer friendship

Teens cats are starting to develop an adult understanding of relationships, and they want them to be equal.

Olwyn helps with our living room reorganization.

They are playing a kind of affection game where we take turns fussing over each other. We have to hold up our end of the game. If we don't see them, we should seek them out. This is how they know it is their turn, and that they should seek us out next time.

Taking turns with affection becomes equally as important when our cat becomes an adult. Whether our cat grew up with us, or not, as adults they are used to figuring things out.

If our relationship is new to both of us, we need to let our cat *know that we know* how to figure things out. Let our new cat see us in action; stocking the food cupboard, fussing over the toy box, seeking them out for a bit of verbal sharing when they are in their favorite spots. Letting our new cat watch our routines is how we will build our new relationship.

If our cat has socialization issues, it is all the more important that this traumatized or feral cat learns new Cause and Effect procedures. Every time we don't do anything bad to them, we have created a new "effect" for them to ponder, and add to their Cat Database. Every time they feel safe in their new hiding place, or get a dish of tasty food, their expectation of disaster is not met.

New causes, new effects.

Cat Science is their game

Cause and Effect is how cats develop their ambushing skills, to surprise the prey by anticipating their movements. Since indoor cats don't have opportunities to express these instincts by hunting, they appreciate us giving them other ways of exercising these mental muscles.

A love of science is also our cat's curiosity at work. They want to know what is in the closed-off room or the seldom opened closet. The contents of a grocery bag or recently arrived box is of great interest. If possible, we should open such things in their presence upon request. Give them the empty, interesting-smelling, box to play in.

Our cat's curiosity is one of the drives that we engage to teach them things.

Where We Go Wrong

Here are some of the ways we humans become our own biggest obstacle to cat training. I know it can be exasperating when the cat annoys, but the answer is never going to be *make the cat stop doing that.*

See a cat? Say something sweet.

Care issue

When cats don't use their litter box, it's often because it is not being maintained properly. When cats knock over our drinks, it's because they don't have access to enough fresh water. If they scratch the couch, it's because we haven't provided an adequate scratching post.

The number one reason for cat misbehavior is us not realizing we aren't meeting their needs. We can solve these issues, and have a happier cat, too.

I have solutions in my Problems section, which is also the Care section. Most of the time, the worst problems come from poorly managed Care.

Medical problem

Cats hide the fact that they are sick. This is a survival instinct, based on not showing weakness to a possible rival or predator. But in our homes, this can mean we have no idea our cat is sick until the cat is very sick.

If a cat cannot think of another way to communicate that they are sick, it can break out as misbehavior. If we find ourselves exclaiming that "They know better," we should then wonder if they are sick. This might be their way of trying to let us know.

Energy buildup

Whenever some local bug is going around and both humans get sick, my home has the additional problem of no one wearing out the cats. The younger and more energetic our cat population, the faster this becomes an issue.

If our cats are getting rowdy, we need to play more and harder. This is where battery operated toys can be our friends, or an actual friend who brings a covered dish can operate the wand toy for a while.

Lack of lanes

If our cats are always leaping and climbing where they shouldn't, we need to ask ourselves where they should be going to do this kind of play. If we can't think of a handy place for them to be, there's your problem.

Cats regard our home as their territory, too. We need to share with our cats. It does everyone a favor if we separate our cats and breakables and keep a clear runway to an adequate cat tree.

Not enough togetherness

If our cat is "bugging" us, they want attention. We must remember that if the cat is complaining about loneliness, *they are always right*.

• When we do provide enough fussing and cuddling, they can stop asking us for it.

We should at least acknowledge our cat's requests for affection with some loving words and gestures. Such entreaties are also their way of sending love to us. Not paying good attention to them at such times is not simply neglect, it is also *rejection*.

Thing We Can't Ignore

There are times we think cats are misbehaving on purpose, but *they don't think of it that way*. They are looking for a reliable way to get us to do something. If they do the **Thing We Can't Ignore**, they get our attention, so they can make their request.

Reverend Jim is a master of this technique. Whatever he was doing when he realizes I am responding to him, that is what he's going to do again. For a while, this tended to be doing things he wasn't supposed to, *because* he knew how to bring me to my feet right away.

We can't let the cat launch themselves onto the chandelier and play with all the sparkly things. Yet, once we have been brought to our feet, *the cat has successfully trained us.*

Now that the cat has trained us, is there anything we can do about it? Of course.

Over time, Reverend Jim has learned how to better communicate his needs and wants to us.

• We can help the cat re-train us.

The next time they play with the thing; we don't react. This forces our cat to reconsider what they are doing to get our attention.

If they do something else, we snap to attention. Our cat will conclude that the *something else* now works better. By continually reacting only to the *something else,* our cat should lose interest in the Thing We Can't Ignore.

If we simply cannot ignore the thing that is being played with, we should consider removing or blocking off access to the thing. It could be that the cat has done us a favor. It was foolish of us to leave that there.

Any time we we have challenged our cat to come up with a new training trigger for us, we need to be alert to something, *anything,* we don't mind reacting to.

- If they show interest in something that won't suffer much from such attention, spring to our feet right away.

Our advantage is that now we know we are being studied. We now know we are choosing what we are going to react to. We can choose wisely.

This is how "cat training" gets done, and is the *only* way cat training gets done. When it is combined with "human training".

Train with Drama

We usually make a task easier if we have more power to apply to it. When we **Train with Drama**, we harness our cat's incredible power of imagination.

Our cats know the tossed sponge ball is not an escaping rodent, or that the wand toy with the waving feathers is not really a bird. We know the video game we are playing is set in an imaginary world.

Our cat's imaginative abilities are part of how they can feel affection for us. They get past our widely differing physical selves and our disparate communications skills to feel genuine regard for us as a "fellow cat".

• In Mimes, I explain how cats act out what they want. We can do that, too.

• Put on a play.

When something in the place is broken, and someone is coming to fix it, I need to explain this to the cats.

• I show sorrow over the broken thing.

• I pretend I hear someone at the door.

• I pretend I am showing someone the broken thing.

• I pretend I am the person fixing the broken thing.

• Repeat a few times until the someone comes.

With this dramatic presentation, I have made this whole situation less upsetting to the cats. They don't like our stress when something is broken, when we have to change our routines because the thing is broken, and especially not noisy strangers in the home.

They will puzzle over all of this until it makes sense. My drama is about acknowledging *what is going on* and also about *what will happen* because of it. It will all make sense when the someone comes and does all the things I pretended they were doing.

Then our cat gets to say to themselves, *Aha. I knew this would happen. My person was trying to tell me.*

The more we play these Fun Games, the better our cat learns our words, because we are "illustrating" our words with our body language.

This is how I can look up from my laptop, tell one of my cats to "Leave it alone," and they will. We have reached a point of trusting communication that they understand my words, and I understand their behavior.

Creating a Visual

Because of the cat's use of Body Language, they have a lot of room in their imagination for seeing things happen. Our own use of pantomime and words — some of which they know — becomes the most powerful way of reaching our cat's mind, what I call **Creating a Visual**.

As we play our Fun Games, we are training our cats to understand our emotions and requests. By looking for our cat's expressions and postures, we can figure out more of what they are thinking.

This becomes as automatic, and enjoyable, as hanging with our friends or enjoying a romantic dinner. We know how they express themselves, and this lets us help them.

Likewise, our cats have eloquent ways of expressing themselves. Once we have learned what they mean by what they "say," we can help our cats *anticipate* and *participate*.

We can help them enjoy our return from work, the unveiling of a new bag of treats, or the play session with a new toy. Once we and our cat have our communications working, we can create the appropriate emotions and attitudes by describing the new thing, and then showing the new thing, all while signaling how we are very happy about the new thing.

My cats find these interactive games of understanding are so enjoyable that if too much time goes by without my playing them, they will lurk about, sending hints that they want to know more. About something.

Now we have a working system that covers all the things which matter most.

Reading the Audience

We need feedback to know if we are getting through to our cats. I find cat ears to be the most expressive part of their face.

Here, Olwyn demonstrates both relaxed, and happy, ears.

—*Happy ears* are when the cat's ears swivel away from their head, and the outer surfaces curve to form a "smile".

—*Puzzled ears* swivel outward, but do not curve. Instead, they flatten, forming a straight line above the cat's head.

—*Unmatched ears* are when one ear is showing one position, while the other ear is doing something different. This is part of a cat using their ears to locate sounds, but it can also mean they are thinking. One ear can "smile", for instance, while the other can show puzzlement. Our cat is, in that instant, "of two minds".

—*Completely folded ears* are often signs that the cat is feeling defensive, and under attack in some way. They will fold them flat back and against their head to protect them from attack.

—*Flickering ears* are like a dashboard light. It says that processing is going on in their brain. When I say a cat's name, and one of their ears twitch, I am getting a visual indicator of their understanding of their name being called.

—*Focused ears* are when they "aim" their ears at the sound they are processing, or simply showing attention, as when we talk to them.

—*Relaxed ears*, when the ears seem to be sliding down off their head, indicate a cat in the midst of a calming activity. Kittens do this when they are tired.

If we think of cat ears as human eyebrows, we will learn to see much more variation in the facial expressions. This can extend into noticing more little clues in their body language.

This will help us learn more Catspeak.

Yours and Mine

The Fun Game called **Yours and Mine** is based on a solid principle of Cat Physics:

• Cat energy cannot be *extinguished*.

• Cat energy can only be *redirected*.

If we think we should simply say "stop that" and expect the cat will stop, we are not understanding what makes the cat do these things in the first place. Cats act on need, and there's no arguing with need.

Our first move in getting our cats to make the right choices should be recognizing the cat energies involved, and diverting them to something else. This can be as simple as throwing a toy to keep kittens out of our computer wires, or as complex as creating something for our cats to play with while we play with our own stuff.

Help our cats learn where the boundaries are by giving them clear areas that belong to them. This satisfies their desire to be near us and keeps them out of trouble.

Much the way kittens cannot resist chasing a thrown toy, our grown cat of any age can have their instincts triggered by objects that they cannot stay away from. If we don't want or can't move these objects, we can apply Yours and Mine.

• if asking our cat to "leave it alone" isn't working

• give the cat something similar that they can safely enjoy

• choose an appropriate substitute

• convince the cat that it is indeed an appropriate substitute

• encourage them to see the substitute as something better

I had a problem with teen Reverend Jim playing with my blind cords. I would glare at him and his face would say, *I know but I can't help it.* My solution was to… give him a blind cord I didn't mind him playing with.

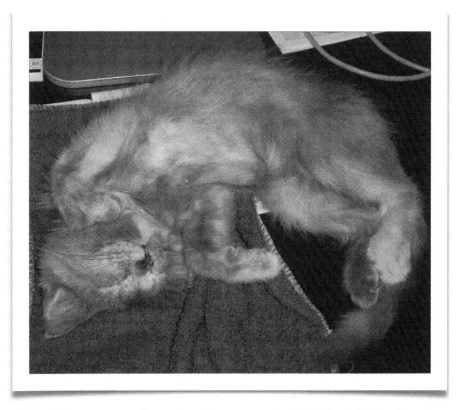

Baby Olwyn was allowed on the computer desk, but she had to stay on her washcloth.

I took a thicker cord (so it wouldn't get tangled) and fastened it to his cat tree. When he would play with the blind cords, I would move him to his cat tree and tell him *this cord* was okay to play with.

It only took a couple of redirects, and he happily played with *his* new toy for months. And left *my* blind cords alone.

Wants are needs

This is how cats have acquired the entirely deserved reputation for stubbornness. It's not that they want to be "bad". It's that they have a strong drive to do whatever it is they are doing.

• We tell the cat, "Don't do that."

• But what if the cat *needs* to do that?

Cat needs can be handled proactively. If one of my cats does something, and I tell them, "Please don't," they usually stop. Because they have something else to play with, or drink from, or perch on, or observe. It is not a high priority for them to have this particular thing when they have so many other things.

But if they do persist, I know they are trying to tell me something. I will need to look at the thing they want and try to figure out what is special about it. Maybe they can play with it in a new way, or it has a quality their other toys do not have. When we offer our cat a substitute, our cat can see it two ways:

• It can be a good, or better, substitute, and thus we are making a friendly gesture. They will be open to switching their interest.

• It is a shabby, obviously inadequate, substitute, and we are putting them on. They will continue to play with what they see as the better option.

It is possible our cat can be simply interested in what we are doing, so we should look for ways to integrate them into the activity. Our cat might love the cord on the computer mouse, which we are constantly moving in a playful way. Give them something with a tail that they can play with while we get things done on the computer.

Often, what we think of as misbehaving is the only way our cat can think of to express a need.

• If they are eating our houseplants, we should grow them some kitty grass.

• If they are playing with wires, they would like some rubber snakes.

• If they are knocking things off tables, they need some bouncy sponge balls.

With better communication, we make this process faster and easier. We can more easily figure out what our cat really needs. We can choose, and offer, better substitutes.

Our cat never does something just to annoy us. They are expressing needs, and cannot help but be be drawn to anything that gives reliable satisfaction.

This is an instance where we actually gain power by giving some to the cat.

• We can get into a battle of wills with the cat.

• Or, we can have a trained and happy cat.

• It's up to us.

Choose the Cues

When we need to convey information to our cat, we have a choice of communication channels. We can attempt direct communication with a combination of verbal and body language. But we can also "cue" our cat by manipulating *elements of the environment* to convey our message.

This can happen by our changing the environment directly, or we can use symbols, which our cat can interpret. Different cats, and different issues, will influence our choice.

If we come home and find that the cat has pulled down a scarf from the pegs on the back of the door and is sleeping on it, we can ask the cat not to. If they continue despite our requests, we have a number of choices to prevent our scarf from looking like a cat slept on it.

- It is always worth figuring out *why* our cat is doing this

- Understanding their *motivation* will help us change this behavior

Our attempts to stop them will run into the fact that they still have that need. We can start storing our scarves in the closet, and then our cat pulls down a whole coat to sleep on. Which means we still haven't solved the need they are expressing.

If this is a *sudden change*, we should ask ourselves *what else has changed*. If we have been working late, this could be our cat expressing their dismay and worry that we are not showing up at our usual time.

Our cat is telling us something through their environmental choices. This behavior is by the outside door. It would mean something different if it was in the bedroom, or the kitchen.

In this case, it might be that our cat is doing this because they miss us. We cannot ask the cat not to miss us.

Change something

The scarf needs to be washed anyway, so if we move it to another place, will the cat move with it? If so, we now know our cat is using the scarf to *symbolize* our presence. We can give them something else for this purpose.

A small blanket or stuffed toy, rubbed on our hair and neck, will imprint this object with our scent.

We can gift the cat with their **Security Object** when we leave, and put it away when we come back.

• Using a Security Object will remind our cat of ourselves when we are away.

• If they are not feeling well it can go with them to the veterinarian's.

What if we moved the scarf and our cat stayed by the door? The cat is sending an *environmental* message. They pulled down the scarf to get some cushioning, but their wish to wait by the door for our return is the actual message. The placement of the object is the important thing, not the object itself.

Our task now is to create a more acceptable place near the door, and get the cat to sleep there. When we put the scarf back, it should be after the cat has accepted our substitute object.

The key to realizing how cats think about their territory:

• It is *physical*, existing in actual space

• It is *mental*, as a model in their minds

• It is *sensory*, as they take in all the sights, sounds, and scents

Extending their territory

Any space left neglected, from a little-used formal dining room to ignored storage areas, can beckon our cat. It is very difficult to convince a cat *this space is vitally needed* and *never to be used* because those two things don't go together in our cat's mind.

For instance, I don't use my dining room table most of the time. So how do I keep my cats off it? It's simple. I don't.

I don't chase my cats off the dining room table for those times *I'm not using it* as a dining room table. When I'm using it as a dining room table, I deliberately make it appear very distinctly different than it does the rest of the time.

Seen here, baby Tristan, with his kitten pillow.

When it is covered with a tablecloth and dishes of food, the cats know they are not welcome there. When I'm not using the dining room table, cats sleep on the blankets which cover, and protect, it. I put tablecloths on the table, and tall items or stacks of plates to signal my cats they are not to jump on the table… now.

Instead of finding a sweet spot to hang out, getting on this new and changed table will get a cat a scolding and maybe even a time out. So they won't get on it. It no longer gives back the response they want.

It has changed. So, to cats, it is easy to see that its purpose has changed.

Since the dining room table overlooks the second favorite window and the cat tree and is close to my writing desk; it is going to be a place cats want to sit on. Ninety percent of the time, I am not using it for any other purpose. When I do want to use it, I would clean it.

People who set their table as though company is imminent and expect the cat to stay off when company never comes (in the cat's mind) are setting up a confusing and upsetting scenario for no real purpose.

We both live here. We can both use the table.

When Cats Are Lawyers

It's true. Cats are lawyers.

We tell them not to get on the kitchen counters, then we find them in the sink. If we are honest, all we can say is, "Well played." Because they aren't on the counter, are they?

Maybe we caught Tristan climbing the back of our favorite chair, in danger of making pulls in the fabric, and we tell them not to do that. We come back in the room to find him perched on top of that chair again. Before we decide he is "being defiant", we might discover that Tristan is now *jumping* to the top of the chair, not *climbing* it.

That, as Tristan knows, and knows I know, is something completely different.

He wanted to sit on top of this favorite chair because it's a great lookout spot, and also because it's my favorite chair. He feels close to me when he is on top of our chair, breathing in our combined scent, and he is sure to be noticed by me when I come to sit in it. He can catnap, keep an ear out for events, and look forward to the enjoyment of my head near his. Tristan loves to have his head on a level with mine.

He agreed not to climb the back of the chair. Isn't that what we objected to? In fairness, we have to admit Tristan has a point. I find for the plaintiff.

- if we have an issue with the *process* the cat is using

- not the *result* they are going for

- cats are smart enough to try an *alternative*

If they have found a way around the rules which removes what we objected to, we should let the cat have what they want. Fair is always fair.

Cats play fair

It's not only *fair*. It lets the cat know that we, too, understand what *fair* means.

Cats have a keen sense of "fair play" which is similar to that of a nine or ten-year-old human child. I base this on the common age when humans become cognizant of fairness, equal treatment, and a sense of individual value and worth.

- There's nothing a cat likes better than a sense of individual value and worth.

- Cats are not motivated by malice or an assertion of dominance.

- They treasure fairness.

In a recent holiday season, Tristan had been caught wrestling with our fabric Father Christmas figure. He had always left it alone since learning it was off limits. This time, he got a pass because Mr WayofCats had absent-mindedly left it on his cat tree upstairs.

But now we had to convey that this concept was still operating, along with an acknowledgement that it was a human mistake that had confused him.

Father Christmas has fully recovered from his wrestling incident. He doesn't really need that bag of gifts actually glued to his back, since it hangs there by itself. He is now resting comfortably on the mantel, which is off limits to cats.

But Tristan was staring at Father Christmas, visibly debating the fine points of this legal issue.

I needed to explain something complicated, so I would have to use my Catspeak.

- This always means *showing*, not *telling*.

Making a special exception

I helped Tristan understand this complicated explanation by *letting him get on the mantel.*

Tristan, in slow stages and with a lot of eye contact, got onto the cat tree and scratching post next to the mantel. This gives a three foot boost to any cat who wishes to explore the mantel, only no one does. Tristan is, usually, totally obedient about leaving the mantel alone.

The rule is, if it is on Tristan's cat tree, it is for him.

But this time is different. Tristan was clearly still curious about Father Christmas's playing status, and also our new length of fake evergreen branches with the lights and berries. He's been cooperative about leaving the mantel alone, but the new decorations and configurations are creating a fixation. He needs to know "what it means" and to do that, he must explore it with his senses.

We've changed the mantel. We've added new things. We've put Father Christmas in a compromising position. Does that mean the rules have changed?

Tristan has to know. Because cats speak Body Language, they are going to ask with their behavior. He doesn't want to study this new thing from a distance. He will not be satisfied with my explanation, though he does appreciate it. He is driven to *experience the thing*.

- once our cat *explores* the thing

- they can *ignore* the thing

We can work against ourselves trying to keep the cats away from things when this will only increase their curiosity. All cats have a strong desire to understand any new element of their environment.

Some cats are satisfied at a distance, others by explanations. But if a cat needs to make this new thing a part of their Giant Sensory Map:

- this *want* will occupy their mind

- until that *need* is satisfied

I let Tristan satisfy himself about all the new things, and reminded him of Father Christmas having an off-limits status since he is now on the mantel. Tristan understood, got down, and left both alone until they were packed away at the end of the holiday season.

Connections

We reach cats through their heart.

They are highly emotional and sensitive.

The way we saved Reverend Jim (aka RJ) was by working with the knowledge that he had a giant heart. He loved us and wanted to please us.

His ability to show gratitude and give cuddling had been his best skill from the beginning. Now he built on that to craft different relationships with everyone in the house.

Turned out, his superpower was being everyone's best buddy.

Their Emotions

One common misconception about cats is that they are not affectionate. Cat Appreciators know this isn't true. We get love every day. The real thing.

Princess Olwyn is a dilute tortoiseshell, with the well-known Tortitude.

Cats are often accused of "working our levers" to get what they want. Consider the times my cat Olwyn will get on my lap and purr and knead my stomach. Often, because she wants something. So I give it to her.

Once she returns to the room from enjoying the something, she doesn't necessarily get back on my lap. This can look... manipulative.

But she didn't act like she loves me because she wanted to get something from me. That is not really what is going on here.

Olwyn is not expressing herself in some kind of linear order. She is reminding me that we love each other; and thus, we do favors for each other.

• She is not *pretending* she loves me to get me to do something.

• She really *does* love me.

Brain and heart

Cat intelligence and cat emotion work together. *They* have to be both thinking and feeling creatures for my methods to work. *We* have to be both thinking and feeling creatures for my methods to work.

Love is not simply the best route to this happy pet relationship. For cats, it is the only way. To understand the cat's heart, we need to understand the cat's brain. Because emotion is how their brain works.

We humans like to think we are rational beings, but it turns out we are more likely acting as *rationalization* beings. We usually decide from an emotional state, and then use our thinking skills to come up with good reasons for doing what we want to do. There's nothing wrong with that, either, as long as we understand this process.

For cats, both their instinctual and their learned emotional responses seem to come from the same place. They rarely second-guess their decisions. In addition, their reaction time is so fast they don't often get the chance to do so.

While cats do have considerable intellectual powers, and it is most useful to know how to access them, their first response is always to go with what has "worked" for them before.

Their natural world rewards fast reflexive action. This works for dinner, safety, and developing their confidence.

We can change a cat's mind, but only at a pace the cat's heart can handle. We should use the same thing that embedded this experience on their brain: *strong emotion*.

Add power

An **Affection Move** can be made at any time, to up the stakes in any Fun Game we play with our cats.

• It's like a D&D roll for Strength.

• This is where the magic happens.

• Love is the strongest emotion of all.

I never doubt that my cats love me. Because they *act* like they love me. Cats are expressing real emotion when they wind around our legs or cuddle on our laps.

This is not a bribe. This is a reminder of our relationship. Exchanging affection is a vital part of our successful cat relationship. There are no other levers to work with.

Cats show up with Affection Move requests all the time, wanting and needing a head rub or a verbal exchange. Even if we are busy, we can always send them our **Look of Delight**.

We are *simply delighted* to catch sight of them. We can make it happen suddenly or let it bloom on our face like a rose. We can say something sweet, but we don't have to.

Flash that Look of Delight and pause long enough to see how their face changes.

Game of Mutual Regard

One of the beautiful things about cats is how they love us in direct response to how much we love them. This leads to the Ultimate Game: the **Game of Mutual Regard**.

It means we cannot let an affectionate gesture go unanswered.

• Our cat rubbed their head on our shin as they went by.

• When we walk through the living room, we rub their head.

• When they get up from their nap, they will show up where we are.

• If we don't see them for a while, we will seek them out at the next opportunity.

When one of us shows affection, the other now feels a bit of pressure to show *we miss them*.

People never complain that kittens are not interactive. Kittens are always wanting to play, often get into things that require intervention, and will show up spontaneously for conversation and cuddles. The boundless reservoir of kitten energy demands our participation, even if it's only to distract them from electrical cords and knickknacks.

People think something bad happens when a cat is no longer a kitten. This is heartbreakingly evident in cat rescue. Kittens show up because no one wanted a cat at all. Then there's another bump in availability; the gangly forms of half-grown cats who are no longer kittens.

At the very moment when cats are developing their individual personalities, when they have learned the rules of the house and have moderated the wild kitten antics, right when they are poised to *deepen the relationship*; people get discouraged and lose interest.

• Because they don't understand the Game of Mutual Regard.

Kittens are too young for the Game. Even a defensive kitten will play in front of us, their inexorable trajectory pinging our radar and promoting a kind of low level attention. All we have to do is sit there, and the kitten will scamper over our foot. For a kitten, this can be contact enough. As the kitten grows older, they become more sophisticated. Little by little, our cat is growing their adult sensibilities, a state in which they can longer ignore our lack of participation.

Tristan, teen cat, with plenty more to give.

All relationships have points where the other party feels they are doing all the work. If we are not alert to our kitten's signals, we won't know when they have grown up enough to begin their first adult moves in the Game of Mutual Regard.

To us, the cat seems to lose interest, because they no longer show up unbidden, they aren't waiting for us at the door, they haven't been moving across our radar screen with the same relentless regularity.

This is when they want us to deepen the relationship. They want us to seek them out, engage them, show them that we find them so compelling, so interesting, so desirable, that we are willing to make this effort. It's not indifference that prompts cats to withdraw a bit.

• In reality, it is a *lack of indifference*.

The cat wants to know if we will miss them when they aren't around. The cat doesn't want to be taken for granted.

So often I hear, "They were so cuddly when they were a kitten. I don't know what happened." Well, I'm sorry to say, *we happened*. When they were so tiny and cute we could hardly help ourselves, we cuddled them, a lot.

Then, as they got older and made their first moves in the Game, we stopped. When we don't understand cats, we might think that now the cat is older, they want to go their own way and no longer need or want affection from we humans.

This is the source of the misconception that makes people say, "Know the problem with a kitten? It grows up to be a cat."

But it doesn't have to be this way. Instead, we can learn the Game.

All great things flow from the Game. Love. Harmony. Humor. Creativity. Peace. The joyous interplay of living beings reveling in each other's company. Without the demands of authority and subservience creating stress and tension.

This is the feature set of cats, and it is a powerful one. It has let cats move into markets far beyond their original niche of rodent control. They command a compelling slice of the companion positions among artists, writers, inventors, scientists, and intellectuals. They have inspired poetry, memoirs, and outright worship across cultures.

They hold the archetype of wisdom and mystery, hidden knowledge and deep secrets.

They ask so little in return.

So when our kitten turns preoccupied, when our older cat appears and only stares at us, these are the subtle signals that say *the ball is now in our court.* If our cat seems to be wanting something; they probably are. They are wanting something from us.

Make the effort to find out what it is. Don't simply run down the mental checklist; bowls full, litter clean, let's move on. There's more to cats than that.

If we find ourselves needing to seek the cat out, *seek the cat out.*

It's our turn.

This is the Game.

Bond of Trust

Our **Bond of Trust** is the magical glue that will keep our cat happy and confident, despite all the confusing information that comes from them living in our human world. If a situation occurs that they have trouble understanding, something their instincts have not equipped them for, our care and affection will be the reassurance they need. Our happy confidence will help them stop worrying about whatever it is.

Cats know, and we should realize, that we have a lot more information about the workings of this world than they do. So we can be an important source of explanations, if they trust us.

Routines are promises

During Olwyn's kittenhood, we acquired a toy that became her favorite; a giant, rubbery, life-like bug. I put it away one night while half-asleep. When I had trouble finding it again, it became a crisis for baby Olwyn.

Because I had promised her she could play with it every time I got home from work. The next evening, when I got home from work and could not produce it, she was frantic. *She had been promised her bug.*

• To our cats, we don't make mistakes.

• Everything we do is on purpose.

It wasn't only that Olwyn wanted to play with her bug. It was also that I had promised she could. *Wasn't I taking care of her any more? Didn't I love her anymore?*

To build a Bond of Trust with our cats, we have to be trustworthy. I found her bug. I had her trust.

When we bring our cats home, we promise that they will be important to us. We will feed them, and provide the kind of places they need, and offer them affection. The more our cat believes this promise, the more upset they will get when they worry that something we promised has changed.

When routines are disrupted our cats will become distressed. It's not simply, as so many think, that they are complaining that their needs are being neglected. They are, and they are right, but that is not all that is upsetting them.

Mithrandir, happy to be near us.

They want to know if our friendship contract has been revoked, if we are upset with them, if we have decided we are not going to keep our promise.

So even if we are rushed or stressed or even frantic with worry, we can help salvage a cat crisis of late meals and inadequate attentions. We do what we can with a little extra reassurance, that extra moment taken to fuss over them. Because while they do need their food and water and litter taken care of, they also need to know that we still love them.

This is truly how we meet all of their needs. For cats, who prefer as much independence as they possibly can, it is a "leap of faith" to turn over important matters like food and water and bathroom needs to humans working the levers in the human world.

Don't take shortcuts

We humans have a tendency to go for the short-term solution, even when this actually complicates potential long-term solutions. We think we can come up with another such "patch" when the down-the-road implications start to develop.

Sadly, that is not how it works. If our short-term strategy messes up our final goal, any possible fixing of the problem has only been made that much more difficult.

When we think our cats cannot decipher our sentences literally, we can feel that it doesn't matter if we try to fool them. We try to get them to accept an inadequate explanation or an outright deception. But then we will have no tools to deal with the unavoidable events in our mutual lives, like vet visits, new foods, new people, redecorating, and moving; all of which will displease our cat.

We cannot fool them into liking such things. But if we start with falsehood in our hearts, we can threaten the Bond of Trust with our cat.

Some cats don't have outings unless they do wind up at the vet, so promising otherwise will not make a dent in our cat's certainty. Pretending the new food is not new, as when we simply dump it in their bowl and hope for the best, is not going to work, either. We don't want to look deceptive, or even clueless, when something is obvious to both of us.

There's other ways we can undermine our happy, useful, connections.

• Do we come home and fuss over the cat, then stop while our cat is still ready for more?

• Do we keep thinking we'll take the time for a nice long play session, and then not actually do it often enough?

• Do we keep chasing our cat off or away from something, instead of figuring out what our cat needs, and giving it to them?

We promised love and care. We need to live up to that, and consistently deliver.

One of the great advantages of cats as pets is that they do wear out or get full or feel satisfied relatively quickly. That swift recharge cycle means several easy opportunities scattered through our whole day… if we make the effort.

So when we say "I love you," there isn't a doubt in the world.

Perspective Tricks

If we don't recognize the impact our size and abilities have on our cat relationship, we will sometimes do the wrong things; and then become puzzled and hurt by the responses we get.

We can play a Fun Game which reassures our cat with **Perspective Tricks**.

To cats, we are giants. Especially when we are standing up and walking around. Imagine looking up at someone who is five stories tall. Let's hope they are smiling at us. Let's hope we know what their form of smiling looks like.

Because most cats are either confident or strive to be so, they won't let on that we can so easily intimidate them, but this lurking element can add tensions to our interactions. There are ways to meet our cat on their own level.

The best way to pet a cat is to *insinuate*. Perspective Tricks help us shift our vast difference in mass and reach into playful ways of acknowledging, and reducing, our cat's instinctive caution.

Cats want us to show restraint and good manners. Here's some Perspective Tricks which will invite the cat closer. Because we are saying all the right things.

• Offer our hand by *not* offering our hand.

• We should use the **Fist of Friendship**.

If we extend our hand for petting in the usual way, it looks like a hand that can grab. Instead, a fist looks like, and is the approximate size of, a cat head. Cats use their heads to express affection, using face contact and forehead bonks to show closeness. So by using our fist, we are using Catspeak to indicate that we do have knowledge of Cat Etiquette.

Our fist can nudge their head, rub their chest, knuckle their chin, and perform all the delicate petting they find so enjoyable. It is also safer. The open hand looks like it could grab a cat, and the outstretched fingers have a tendency to poke ears or eyes. Using it sends the wrong message.

Up our game and let the cat *pet themselves* with our Fist of Friendship. That way, they control where and how fast, and we look delightful and charming. Like someone they would like to know better.

Offer smallness

All the best approaches to cat petting works because we *humble ourselves*. We should move in ways which make us seem smaller. By using different parts of our body to approximate the cat's size, we convey a sense of equality between us. Cats love that.

The most versatile Fun Game based on this kind of enjoyable pretending is an Affection Move I call **The Shift**.

Use this move by acting in a way which suggests we and the cat have equal size and weight. Get down on the floor at their level, be patient enough for them to make their way over to us, be loving enough to see affectionate gestures from the cat's point of view, not ours.

This is how we create cats who long for such closeness, and gift us with the meshing of our personal space. We can simply lie still, use our voice to express affection, and let our cat make all the petting moves. One of the most polite ways we can express affection is to encourage them to pet us, instead of always making ourselves the one who pets.

• The Shift works for any cat.

Timid cats find their confidence increased when they interact with us in a way that does not make a point of our human size and power. Smokepuff used to love this move because hugging could overwhelm him. It also works when a cat's understanding of their surroundings is still not reliable, such as the early days with severely neglected Reverend Jim.

This move works equally well with cats whose problem is a tendency to be defensive and fearful. They are soothed when we present a less threatening presence. The cat who tends to be too rough will scale back; once we do.

Get down to their level.

Even cats who have good relationships will love this move because to them, it's funny. Our cat knows we are actually larger and more powerful, but they also know we are pretending not to be.

Especially for shelters

When I observe and interact with cats in shelter cages, I realize I appear as a **Big Giant Head**. But I use this to my advantage. I put my hands behind my back and keep my body out of the picture as much as possible.

When we see our cat in a relaxed posture at home, approach them very slowly, with our hands behind our back and our head forward. Whisper their name in a happy tone, and tilt our head slowly from one side to another.

By concentrating our cat's attention on our head, we become smaller and thus, more friendly. We are not doing hands that grab or feet that kick; both reactions too many strays have learned to fear.

If we have never tried to pet the cat except as some looming, leaning-over entity, we might be surprised at the difference it makes to our cat. It's not about how big or small we or the cat may be, it's how much effort we will each put in towards expressing equality.

That's the hidden dimension we are able to bridge. Being bigger than the cat, we should scale back to express an equal playing field of affection. The more cunning our play, the more we engage the cat's thinking, and trusting, side.

We both get what we want.

There's three Affection Moves which can be the most elusive or puzzling. Here's how we can get it for ourselves, or why we aren't getting it.

Nose Boop

This is the adorable move where we touch the tips of our noses together.

This is a friendship gesture which kittens submit to when young but comes with ramped up respect requirements as they grow up. Even my cats who love booping don't want me running up to them and throwing my face in their direction.

• They want to be wooed.

If we creep closer and closer, pitching our voice softer and softer, and telling them how much we love them, our cat will find themselves *wanting* more closeness. Because we are being so nice.

The closer we get, the slower we move, the more our cat feels compelled — by the Law of Reciprocity — to return all these lovely feelings we are creating in their heart. As our face gets closer, they should start reaching out with their own face.

This is a delicate maneuver. Remember that our head probably weighs as much as our entire cat. Be gentle.

Most failed Nose Boops are from not respecting the cat's dignity enough for them to feel comfortable. The more we mess this up, the more reluctant they feel to be drawn into this Affection Game.

Earn that Nose Boop.

Lap Cat

Many people consider Lap Cat to be the height of cat love, and it's either/or.

• Either the cat is always on our lap

• Or they don't love us

The truth, as always, lies somewhere in the middle.

Lap sitting is a delightful form of closeness, but individual cats might not regard it as highly as we do. One serious barrier to lap cat enjoyment is that this is *not a stable surface*. Cats will stay for a while to be petted, or a long while for a nap, but we are going to have human needs that make us at least shift our weight, or have to get up.

What helps is:

• Announce imminent lap cat time, as we get ready to watch or read something

• Spread a blanket on our lap to make the surface look smoother

• Shy cats will appreciate a box on our lap for even more stability

• Commit to enough time to make it worth both our whiles

That picture of us with a happy cat on our lap is a lovely picture, but it's not a moving picture. It's no wonder cats might prefer snuggling *next to us*, instead.

That way, they can stay in one spot, all relaxed and with their limbs arranged the way they like, instead of being moved all the time.

This isn't like taking a lap-desk on and off our laps, which stays the same shape. Cats, with their flexible backbone and reactive limbs and highly cranked nervous system, don't like being rearranged.

Additional issues with lap cats:

—*Might be long.* Tristan is too long and lanky to sleep curled up on my lap. So, if I am reclining in bed, he will appear to stretch out over my entire torso.

—*Might be sensitive.* This was Smokepuff's issue. If I was curled up in the recliner with a book, I would stay still long enough for him to settle in. But one leg cramp or indrawn breath and he was gone. He interpreted the tiniest details as a signal for him to leave.

—*Might be uncertain.* The lap cat position is one of great trust, which is why humans prize it. But if our cat is still getting used to us being so close, lap is too much, too soon. Trying to make them stay will make this option even less attractive.

—*Might be sudden.* Start small, like sitting next to them on the couch. They don't have to move, we can watch or read something, and both of us enjoy the company.

Mind Meld

Or as I call it, the Vulcan **Mind Meld**. We press our foreheads together.

Olwyn, open to a Mind Meld.

This is not as delicate as Nose Boop, but it's an even greater gesture because cats consider their faces to be highly vulnerable. (Like their bellies, which is why they are touchy about that.) In Nose Boop it touches and we're gone, but Mind Meld should *last*.

The affectionate head butt we can get from our cats reaches its highest form when we Mind Meld with each other. It can make things easier if our cat is on a shelf or the back of the couch, where our foreheads can easily meet.

Moving in for the full Mind Meld is a process, like Nose Boop, which must be done slowly. But once completed, there's a meditative calm about it, and if our cat is purring, the sound will fill our heads.

I see Mind Meld as a move of utter equality. A meeting of two minds.

Shaping the Response

Another advantage of expanded trust and communication is how this helps us guide our cats. We help them towards proper responses to our shared environment by modeling the proper attitude towards new things and puzzling events.

I call this **Shaping the Response**.

We should always be thinking of ways to Shape Their Response when we offer them something new, rearrange the furniture, shift our own work and play schedule, or even when something startling happens. The better our relationship with our cat and the more trust we have in each other, the more easily we can let them know what to think about new things. This lets our cats file this information away in their Cat Database.

Whether we are offering a new food or changing an established routine, our cats will always look to our reaction to help them form an opinion. They know they are living in our human environment, not their natural, cat, one.

We don't have to dread introducing our cats to the new couch or the new Significant Other if we remember that we can help them understand that we regard this as a *really good thing*. We use happy tones in our voice, act quietly excited about the something that is about to happen, and unveil the new thing with lots of fuss, using their names.

This conveys: *This new thing is for them. It's awesome. It's a gift.*

Local expert

I became aware of this highly useful tendency when I was running my amateur cat rescue, with double digits of cats routinely flowing through the house. Something would happen... and many cat heads would swivel my way. *What did I think?*

Once I realized I was being regarded as a local expert on whatever it was, I began conveying my attitude through exaggerated body language. I would mime the emotion I wanted the cats to access when they thought about this new thing.

Most of them did begin to think that way. They would then model the proper response to the cats who were not so fluent in Human.

The more a cat expects something bad to happen, and then something bad *does not happen*, the more this new information will influence their attitude.

Threat assessment

Much of our cat's finely tuned, highly cranked, nervous system is about being on the lookout for threats. Even if their humans don't see any.

We need to know our cats to gauge the information they want to tell us.

—*Trigger level.* Some cats have their alarms set Very High, like Tristan. The tensing of my body before a sneeze is enough to send him racing to another room, even though a few minutes later, (whether I sneezed or not,) he will likely be back.

Knowing how our cat reacts to possible threats helps us evaluate their source. Because we don't always know where they think the threat is coming from.

—*Trouble source.* An important part of figuring out what is upsetting our cat is knowing where their sensitive spots are. When his friends downstairs went on vacation, and allowed another couple to stay there, Tristan noticed *there were new people living there!* He raced up to me with his eyes darting around, then tensely crouched on the bookcase at eye level.

Tristan's imagination became the source of thoughts which deeply upset him. I had to figure out what he was reacting to in order to soothe him. I wouldn't have been able to do that if I didn't know the depth of his emotional ties, and how much he liked our neighbors.

—*Redecorating.* Cats might find furniture rearrangement, different noises, or even new smells, to be highly upsetting. For instance, brand-new shower curtains, out-gassing when they come out of the package, have an effect on cats which gets them over-charged and wild-eyed.

With our cat's super-senses, they are going to notice such changes almost instantly. Help by explaining what is going to happen, what is happening now, and what might have happened at appropriate times.

—*Teach self-soothing.* One of the most valuable bits of training I ever did was teaching young Tristan how to self-soothe. When he would wake me up at night because everyone was asleep and he was sad and lonely, I would cuddle him against my chest, neck, or hip to show him how he could feel connections even if I were asleep.

Soon, he would seek out these spots and cuddle himself against me when he felt lonely. Later, he would choose the curve of my knees as his special spot for sleeping with me, and didn't even wake me. He had learned how he could take care of this need, by himself.

Shaping the Response lets our cats know what we think of that thing, which can reassure them that it is, after all, no big thing.

Cat Time, Human Time

One of the major ways Human Time works so much faster, for us, is how we have access to better information. We are working in a human world, using human things. *We know the backstory.* This is only one of the many circumstances where our perception of time, and our cat's perception of time, will not be in synchronization.

We come home from the grocery store and think it will only take a few minutes to get our shopping put away, and then we'll open the can of the favorite flavor. But our cat, who ate their least favorite flavor for breakfast this morning, has been waiting all day in the hopes something better will appear. They don't want to wait a few more minutes.

It's been a whole week of the new cat quarantined in the spare bathroom, and we are more than ready to have our normal routines back again. Our cat has been asked to share their territory with a total stranger, and they aren't ready yet.

Their people would like to hurry them up over what a cat sees as very big things, like changing their food or adding another cat. Their people might think playtime should be over already when their cat is still getting revved up.

To understand the kind of time sense cats use, it can be helpful to understand what parts they are good at, like *duration*. They can keep track of how long it takes their prey to reappear in a certain spot. Then a hunting cat will be able to tell when they have waited for that period of time. This keeps them from wasting time on a hunting situation that is now unlikely to pay off.

They are not good at exact measurements of time, which is a human thing. Daylight Savings Time throws them off. Their usual cues which tell them what time it is, or what time it should be, are still operating in a pre-clocks-adjusted way. We can intervene by showing them the clocks and explaining why we are adjusting them; this will let them know something is changing.

Give them signals

They are good at schedules which have clear, cat-recognizable, cues. We can be amazed that our cats are ready at the door when we come home, but their hearing is much better than ours. They can recognize our car before it pulls into the driveway.

They are bad at schedules with cues that they cannot discern. Our cats will get into less mischief while we are gone if they have plenty of different diversions. They are bad at being bored because, as with small children, a terrain without interest stretches on forever.

They are adding up all kinds of cues we don't notice; because we do have clocks and watches. Cats have guesses and clues and cues. If training seems to be going slowly, we need to remind ourselves that we are probably not seeing this situation the same way our cat is.

By looking at a problem from someone else's perspective, we often find the solution.

Love of routine

The importance of **Cat Routines** cannot be underestimated. Cats love routines.

Mithrandir, our recovering feral, finds schedules soothing. He loves milling around the kitchen in the mornings while I prepare the cats' breakfast, but if I add making tea to take to work, this will distress him until this new part of the routine is no longer new.

On the other hand, Olwyn will head toward the commotion, so she can take over and fix things. Even if it is something that is not in her skill set. To make Olwyn happy, we have to tell her she "has it all under control."

She is a cat who gets the most distressed when we leave for appointments that are not part of the routine, or have repair people come. She understands "having friends over" but not strangers who make strange noises in her stuff.

Mithrandir spent his first year with us working on
What Comes Next.

When cats think they know what will happen, and then it does, they feel that they are in control. They feel they understand how things work in their world. They need our help to make all this make sense to them. They need to know our partnership is reliable.

So if we are going to be late, we should tell the cats. If the routines are going to be scrambled for a while, we should alert them to that fact.

If we have make them wonder *what will happen next*, let's make it a pleasant surprise, instead of a surprise.

Conveying Meaning

Our Bond of Trust has other uses. We also might be surprised by how well the proper kind of **Cat Explanations** will work to transmit our *meaning*.

Cats will never learn all the complexities of our human language. We can't explain things to them the way we can to a fellow human. But *trying to explain* can advance our cause more than we might ever guess.

It is probably my most controversial cat advice. I listen to people coping with an overstressed cat, and often they are doing a lot of the right things. Then, at the end, I have to ask, "Have you tried explaining things to the cat?" (Turns out, a person can hear side-eye.)

But then they bring themselves to try it… and report that it works. I'm all about whatever works. By so doing, we realize how good cats really are when it comes to sending and receiving information from other beings.

In nature, cats would be crouching in wait, figuring out what the prey will do, anticipating all the moves it might make to get away, and how they would counter such behavior. Cats like to hang out with us, in part, to study our moves and see where they can fit themselves into our routines.

The framework of routines

Whenever a cat imagines where their prey will be for ambush purposes, they are working abstractly, using a flexible conceptual model to stand in for the reality of their next meal. Cats can learn our schedule, like James Bond did when I was in college, even though this was a pattern that changed every semester, and was also different in between.

Having solid Cat Routines helps our cats exercise all those hunting instincts and reflexes. They monitor activity, anticipate the next few steps, and figure out where to insinuate themselves into the flow of action. Then, it's ambush time.

It's basic Pavlovian reflex for them to come for dinner at the sound of a can opener, but what about when my cats would run the electric can opener to summon me to the kitchen? That's working with *concepts*.

By talking to our cats with a lot of facial expression and other body language, our cats learn more words. This is how they learn which word fits into something they would express in their cat language, or what human facial expression creates the same feeling in their brains. The more we practice this, the better we both get.

Which is why I don't explain only when there is a crisis. I explain things all the time. It's a fine reason and excuse to talk to my cats, and it benefits us all when crises do occur.

They understand signals. They don't know what "work" means. But they do know the word "work" signals a shift in my presence, time, and attention.

Give an explanation

They now have an explanation for our possible absence and inattention. It doesn't matter if they understand web design or customer service or whatever we do at work. They don't have to understand economics or vehicles to understand that we go out and sometimes we come back with food and treats and toys. These are human concerns, but now they have a box to put all this activity in, one that gives them a grasp of fundamentals.

Don't make it boring when we get out the wand toy for a play session. Ask if anyone is interested in the phrase "wand toy". Wander around where the toy is kept. Examine it closely, and if it needs putting together, all the better. By the time the toy is actually deployed, our cat is wound up with excitement and will get extra enjoyment from the entire process. They will learn the phrase *wand toy*.

Points for effort

Remember that cats do give points for effort. Sharing sincere words and gestures about our compassion and caring soothes our cats. Whatever is going on, we are on their side and working to make things right, somehow.

Mithrandir learned what the words "Mouser Mix" meant, with his favorite of our herbal cat toys.

Which is the simple magic of explanations. Whether our cat understands a lot or a little, our cats look for signals from us. We don't have to get them to understand the details. We are taking care of the details.

Whenever we make explanations, we are conveying good signals about the present crisis, be it a plumbing problem that will require strangers doing noisy things or a career change that will mean all these boxes are going somewhere else, and so will our cats.

By explaining whatever-it-is to our cats, we are automatically sincere while conveying the important message, "It's cool, the humans got this." Honesty and accuracy is simply the best way to convey the message. We should keep it simple and we probably need to do it more than once, but actually doing it?

It shows we care. Which is the best message of all.

Joy of Anticipation

We and our cats should share mutual, enjoyable, Cat Routines. Cats prefer a predictable existence. Reliable Cat Routines appeal to our cat's sense of *anticipation* and *participation*.

• They need to know our partnership is reliable.

Disruptions need to be signaled with **Cat Alerts**. The more events we plan and share with our cat, the more we develop the power to summon them for various purposes. In our household, there's treat time, nip time, cuddling-on-the-bed time, a-closet-door-is-open time, and many others.

Like humans, cats can enjoy suspense, as long as they are confident the surprise will be a pleasant one. If our cat's anticipation turns to frustration, we've let the suspense go too far. But most of the time, this can turn into another fun game to play with our cat. Because cats absolutely love looking forward to something good about to happen.

To put this into practice, use the Three Rules of Non-fiction.

• 1. Tell them what we are about to tell them

• As we get better at cat communication, our cat will be better able to anticipate the discussed action.

• 2. Tell them

• Now, something happens. The thing we told them about.

• 3. Tell them what you've told them

• Now we discuss it with quiet excitement.

This mirrors our cat's natural ability in studying, anticipating, and ambushing their prey. They will appreciate being warned that something will happen, even if they don't know what they were being warned about.

By creating situations where they understand how these routines have a beginning, middle, and end, we help them deal with living in our unpredictable, human, world.

If our cat doesn't know how to interpret the emotion the humans are displaying, it can make them anxious.

Embrace the new

This helps us handle their resistance to change. This essential counterbalance to their bright and curious minds is a vital safety measure. In the wild, *the new* was probably dangerous, and possibly hungry.

The best way to handle our cat's resistance to change is to help them understand how we view the change, and try to get them more into alignment with our own attitudes. We can use their enjoyment of anticipation to enlist their participation, since cats are highly sensitive to our moods.

We often inadvertently sabotage ourselves by being anxious about how the cat will accept the new companion or the move to the new house. The cat will pick up our nervous mood, and become nervous themselves.

So let's talk about the new arrangements with a light heart and a lilting voice. Create moments, with props, where we can bring up the subject, and use these props later, as the new situation is evolving. We have the power to **Shape Their Response**.

• If we let them make up their minds without positive feelings from us, they will err on the side of caution.

• Encouraging them to investigate, at their own pace, will work better than by trying to force the response we want.

For new food, offer them both foods for a while, and mix the two in varying proportions. Get them ready for a move by creating a box for their stuff, and make an emotional show over where their box goes in the new house. All of these strategies won't overload their minds with too much to consider all at once. Give them time to think.

As I always say of them, *If the idea is mine, I will be fine*. If we can display the situation in a way that lets them *choose* to like it, they are that much more open to acceptance.

If their cat bed or scratching post has become so well-used we long to replace it, don't throw out the old one before we get the new one. Have both around, but the new one is spiced up with catnip or there are treats in it. The old one can be cleaned, which makes it lose its scented appeal.

It is less attractive than it used to be. This lets our cat decide for themselves that the new item is better.

It takes a little planning and thinking to create the right situation for our cat to accept new things. But we can do that. Aren't we supposed to be the more intelligent creature?

The Three Principles of Cat Decision Making

• 1. The love of the status quo.

• If things are not actively horrible, then things are fine the way they are.

• 2. The strongest impulse is caution.

• It's hard for a cat to grasp that they can get in trouble by *not* doing something.

• 3. The default is negativity.

• If they have no previous experience to draw upon, they figure they won't like it.

The key to convincing cats, who dislike anything new, is to hang in there with the new thing. Until it is no longer new.

Time Management

Do we know how to spend time with cats? We will join the cats in their favorite amusements. We will also see our cats join us in our daily tasks.

When Olwyn was a kitten, she "helped" Mr WayofCats with his daily sweeping of the kitchen. She hung around the dustpan when she decided it was time to take it out of its holder, chased the broom, and talked about the shared activity. This is not a fast way to sweep the kitchen.

But if Mr WayofCats and I insisted on efficiency, we would all miss out on the fun. While I love curling up with a book (or a device) and a kitty, that's only the beginning. The more we find daily routines where our cats enjoy interacting with us, the more our cats get the amusement, puzzles, and attention they crave.

So create a kitchen Outpost for our cat, and we have company while we make dinner. Get ready for our day, together, and we leave our cat feeling loved while they are away from us all day. Our maintenance tasks and homecoming rituals and bedtime routines are all places where we can welcome our cat's participation.

Likes to watch

If we have a cat who loves to monitor the things we do, we have a **Supervisor**.

Curiosity, observation, and companionship are the very heart of Supervision enjoyment. So when we make egg salad, or cross stitch a sampler, or add new memory to our computer; these can all be utterly fascinating activities which our cat will want to... supervise.

Supervisors not only want to have things work right, they want to figure out what working right means and what the thing does. This is part of their love of figuring things out. If there are any gears turning anywhere, a Supervisor cat wants to watch and learn.

Other beings in the house can be seen as wheel cogs, too. If we are interacting with our kitten, dog, or spouse, and feel cat eyes upon us; it's our local Supervisor, learning something they hope to put to good use.

From the cat's point of view, we are master manipulators of our environment. They often like to see a master at work. Let them be company for us, but tell them what tools or materials are paws-off for them. Sometimes, though, we are busy, and only want to *hit the pause button*.

If the problem is they are trying to get into our activity, we can end it most easily by satisfying, instead of frustrating. If they show curiosity, hold something out to them, for the closer look or sniff they are wanting. This will often satisfy them, and they can continue watching without interfering.

Pick a Spot

Give them a chance to be our companions. If we tell them to **Pick a Spot**, they know they are supposed to choose an Outpost (which we have provided) and stay out of the way.

This works the other way, if we are working with something they regard as their own. We might expect this when we are washing their food dishes or cleaning the litter.

But this same *ownership feeling* can come up with chairs they like to sleep on, their favorite window, or even our disassembled computer.

It can even be something they know is important to us. They wish to express concern about the gutted computer chassis or the broken lamp.

Provided, of course, they had nothing to do with it getting that way.

Cat's point of view

Keep in mind that we know more about the baffling things we do than our cat does.

• Some forms of *busy* don't look busy to the cat.

Sitting motionless and staring at something, with occasional small movements of our hands, looks about the same as staring into the distance and twiddling our thumbs. It is frustrating to be deep into our thesis, a computer game, or figuring out the locked room murder... only to have a cat fling themselves into our field of play.

But if they are lonely, they might figure we are lonely too. If we can, some sweet talk or chin rubs will let them know we notice them.

• If they are asking for something when we can't stop right now, give them a time (point at a clock or our watch) when we will get up and get them what they want.

• Then do it.

• This will train them to trust our follow-through.

• They can learn patience.

Getting the cat to understand "Not Now" will only be accomplished if we say it and practice it. We meet a request with a verbal phrase, which can even be a Monty Python-esque "Wait for it..." as I like to do.

Then, if they subside, we pause... and then comply. As we stretch out the times in between pausing and paying close attention to them, always faithfully returning to be at their service when we said we would, we build our Bond of Trust with our cats.

Curiosity is a strong motivator for all cats, but we might not realize that it is the addition of *ourselves* to a task which can make it fascinating. If we can come up with ways for the cats to enjoy things we enjoy, this is that much more time we can spend together.

The presence of our cats can turn chores into playtime. One of the many magic tricks they offer.

Rewrite the Role

Here's some of the most common ways people make Non-Affection Moves:

• The *Deadly Belly* is often regarded as a trap. Dogs like having their bellies vigorously rubbed on the slightest pretext. Cats don't.

• *Instead:* Admire the belly from afar. We can pretend we are going to pet the belly… and then we don't. We can point to the belly, and wiggle our fingers as though we are petting the belly; but we are not.

• The *Smacked Head* is when a cat extends their head to show interest. We stick our big palm in their face and bounce it on the top of their head. We think we're being affectionate. The cat thinks we are threatening a beatdown.

• *Instead:* Use our Fist of Friendship to gently rub their chest or face.

• The *Air Rescue* is when we grab the cat around their chest and levitate them. For humans, suddenly being yanked upward by our collarbones is a good thing when it's our fifth day at sea and the rescue helicopter has arrived. But it's always a terrible way to pick up our cat.

• *Instead:* Scoop them up while supporting their weight.

Our cat might be shy about being picked up because we're always doing it the wrong way. We should use both hands; or forearms, if we have a large cat. Slide one hand under their chest, and use the other to scoop up their powerful hindquarters. Their "foot" actually extends all the way back to their heel, which is the first bend up the leg.

Cats walk on their toes, (which is why declawing should be a crime), and we can cup their paws, or their entire back feet, to help support their weight when we pick them up.

If we have been petting in ways which are not getting us the results we want, it's time to start things from scratch. Since our hands are the culprits in these unsatisfying petting sessions, we should "recast" the role of Hand in our interactions with our cat.

Meet the new Hand

One trick that can help our cat look at Hand differently is what I call **Secret Hand**. This is a game where I sit near a cat, or rest my hand near a cat, and then Hand sort of sneaks over for a bit of touching, all by itself.

My hand is much smaller than the cat. It is only threatening when it has the force of my whole person behind it. A hand acting on its own is intriguing. Because I let it crawl over from beneath the cat, not descend from above, it looks less threatening.

This is not something which works with kittens or cats who are prone to pounce on what looks like a toy. We are not trying to teach them our hand is a toy. But if we have a cat who has been apprehensive about us trying to pet them, Secret Hand can help with their worries.

An important advantage of Secret Hand is that it uses the kind of Perspective Tricks our cat understands.

Cats can have a wonderful sense of humor, and pretending that our hand is operating on its own is a type of physical humor they seem to get. They know it is our hand, but here it is, acting as though it is an independent being.

Offering Secret Hand can reduce their anxiety, like the way we humans find a good laugh can make us feel better in a tense situation. Then they are more likely to see my hand, and offer of petting, as the soothing thing I mean it to be.

Right kind of teasing

If our cat is apprehensive about any approaching hands, we can work with that. What I call **Villain Hands** is a trust game.

We spread our hands out as though we are going to grab the kitten or cat, and we advance very slowly, and only slightly menacingly. By doing it in the opposite way of trying to grab them, most cats will appreciate the joke we are playing. It is mildly thrilling, like a cat version of a scary movie.

If our cats are frightened, we can play Villain Hands from across the room, where there is no possibility of actually grabbing them. This is how we get them used to the new role Hands will be playing in our relationship.

Some cats run away as soon as we try it, and we must stop this game until they feel more confident. Other cats, like Tristan, will not even grasp that we are playfully threatening them. Tristan sits there, waiting for the hands to swoop in and pet him. *Why else are they there?*

Harmless teasing is the kind where both parties are in on the joke.

Trust Games

Here are two instances with Tristan which illustrate the many faces our Bond of Trust can have.

Mithrandir the Magician was rescued at five weeks, adopted at ten weeks. His litter was born to a feral mother who had already passed on her untamed attitude.

He asked me to play with him using the big living room cat tree. I throw small toys at the top of the tree, and he races to the top, perches on the top shelf, and tries to catch them. Furry mice, sponge balls, and **our herbal cat toys** are all favorites.

But this time, after playing for a while, I picked up a toy ball the size of a soccer ball. This isn't a cat toy. Was I really going to throw this at Tristan?

For the first time, Tristan played this game. I could see his face go still as he was confronted with playful teasing that he understood. Almost immediately, I put the ball down, laughed, and let him figure out that I was only playing, after all. He gave me a big Cat Kiss. He liked this game.

We've reached the point where we can play Villain Hands with Mithrandir, our kitten with feral issues, and he gets it. He looks up with those always-slightly-apprehensive eyes, and lets the hands come closer and closer... and pet him.

Outline the trust

People who do enjoy the right kind of teasing come away with a better sense of each other's boundaries. This works for our cat, too.

This is the progression we can do with any Affection Move. Start small and far away, and get closer and closer with each round of the game. If our cat feels apprehension, and then figures out they don't need to, their wary feeling will get smaller each time.

If we think of cat paws as cat hands (and I do) we can think of ways to exchange affection with our cats the same way humans do with each other.

When one of our cats is lying on a bookcase or other surface with their paw hanging in the air, I like to come over, whisper softly to them, and put my hand under their paw, lifting it up a little and playing with it. Most of the time, they will open their eyes a slit, or flick their ears, enjoying the contact.

By whispering to them before I touch them, I have given them the gift of *expectation*. Cats are so sensitive we should always move slowly and carefully when we are first offering affection, and check on their receptivity.

Give them a hand

Among humans, "hand play" comes with some important rules. From handshakes to walking hand in hand, we signal our relationships with each other. We can't make someone shake hands with us or drag them along without some kind of bad feelings coming along for the ride.

Likewise, our cats need to be happy about **Paw Play** for it to be seen as a loving, intimate gesture.

By placing my hand under a cat paw, I am creating the same "feel" as though that cat had put their paw on my hand. This makes it the opposite of an offensive move, by any definition.

I let my cat's paw rest on my palm, the back of my hand, or on my fingers, but I don't overwhelm their paw sensors with a full clamp-down. This implies some sort of coercive move that I don't want to include as a part of this experience.

I can gently enclose the paw with my hand, but never in any way where they cannot withdraw it at any time. Tristan will pull his paw from my loose fist, and then put his paw on top of my hand.

I will let him enjoy this sense of being the initiator, then I will slowly rotate my hand to enclose his again. We can do several slow motion rounds of this loving game.

• Never lose track of how much input comes in through our cat's paws

• cats have receptors in the visual part of their brain that are connected to their paw whiskers

• they can "see with their feet"

Many cats love Paw Play, because it is a perception shift where it is more likely to be seen as a gesture between equals.

Tristan likes to drape himself over my shins and grab my big toe with both front paws. This lets him Paw Play in a situation where he can feel that we are of similar size, by matching body parts on that basis. This is similar to the way our Fist of Friendship is about the size of a cat's head, and can be used to make affectionate gestures the way cats do.

These are body language moves. It is Catspeak.

Power of Spoiling

One of the best things about the human/cat relationship is that we can spoil each other, and only *good things* happen as a result.

This is not the case with all relationships. While I also try to spoil my dogs, children, friends, and romantic partners, none of these have the purity and ease of cat/human spoiling.

Baby Tristan, with one of our herbal cat toys.

Only cats, with their commitment to equality, allow for the full flower of mutual spoiling from the very beginning of the relationship.

Make a Fuss

When we give our cats things, we should fuss over them. When people ask me what I mean, I respond, "You know... **Make a Fuss**." By surrounding our gift with happy feelings and cheerful voices, our cats regard this gift as a sign of our high esteem. Which it is.

If we try to force compliance by becoming a punishing presence, our cat will not "learn the lesson" we are trying to convey. We think we are communicating "fear of kitchen counters" but they won't become afraid of the kitchen counters, they will simply get on them when we are not around

• They will fear *us*.

• They will avoid *us*.

The only thing we are teaching the cat when we frighten them is that we are unpredictably frightening.

I am reminded of this when I share a funny story about my cats, and someone takes offense at how I treat them. How *well* I treat them.

Spoiling is good for the cats, and their gratitude is paid by them spoiling me, with affection. Which Cat Skeptics don't believe in, anyway.

Crossing the invisible line

I come in for some scorn because I have the Litter Robot and cat fountains, which provides running water the way my cats like. I even let the cats share my Chromebook, so they can watch cat videos when winter has made the outside landscape less interesting.

If I were to refer to it as our backup laptop, which spent its time sitting on a closet shelf, no one would bat an eye. But if I describe it as the cat's Chromebook, some would get indignant and act huffy, like letting my cats watch videos on Youtube is snatching food from the mouths of starving children.

The way we use it is an example of Yours and Mine. The cats can use "their" screen while the humans use theirs, and everyone is happy. These days, the Internet brings us so much, and is so valuable and needed, having backup devices is not that different from everyone in the home having access to bowls for their food.

Loud and proud

What seems to upset Cat Skeptics most is when I display behavior and words that indicate I value my cats. How dare I. Cats are not supposed to be abused, in this view, but they are "not worthy" of any aspect of care above the minimum. If I do, critics tell me I am valuing cats above people.

If I let my cats sleep on the bed and exiled Mr WayofCats to the floor, this might have some validity, but I spoil Mr WayofCats, too. Not only do I let him sleep on the bed, I get him food he likes to eat and surprise him with books and music occasionally. As he does with me. As we do with our cats, when it comes to favorite flavors and cat toys.

We take care of our little family as well as we can afford, and in addition we support charities which help animals and children. I think most of us do the best we can with what we've got.

What doesn't make any sense is cutting corners where living beings are hurt as a consequence, or trying to drop good causes into a pit for them to fight it out in some kind of winner-take-all scenario.

As these things go, spoiling our cats is quite reasonably priced. Especially when we consider the "bang for the buck" we receive from such pursuits.

My reward for spoiling the cats is multiplied many times in my joy at their joy, and in the increased affection, cooperation, and interaction I get in return.

• We can't go wrong with spoiling.

The more we spoil our cat, the more obligated they are, and the more eager to treat our requests with respect. Likewise, when our cat spoils us, we want to spoil them more.

It's a lovely system which cannot be improved upon.

Rules of Indulgence

For example, I had a blog reader write in:

> Today a small shipment from Amazon arrived. The box was the puuuurrrrrfect size for a cat. I absent-mindedly left the empty box on the dining room table. Normally, T– never goes on the dining room table, but later I heard a rustle, turned around and T– was up there investigating the box.
>
> The instant he saw me he scurried down. I spoke to him soothingly and put the box on the floor and he promptly occupied it.
>
> My wife said that I am letting T– get away with too much and I should have punished him. My thoughts are:
>
> 1. Punish him how? He already knew he should not be up there. Anything I did would simply have made him wary of me.
>
> 2. It was ME that should have been punished because I created something irresistible to T–.

I thought T–'s person had handled it exactly right.

The husband is acting on his knowledge of, and respect for, his companionship with T–. He sees T– as his *friend*.
The wife is acting from knowledge of a pet as something which needs to be controlled. She sees T– as still a *wild animal*.

How we view them

They are each acting from their own relationship with T–. If we treat our cat as a wild animal who needs to be controlled; if we see them as an unpredictable being who needs to be firmly reminded of boundaries; if we do not trust our cat — we will not have a friendship with them.

They will be, for all intents and purposes, a wild animal.

This is why what some people call "cat training" is so frustrating and unsuccessful.

• Human's point of view: "The cat is still doing it. It is defying me."

• Cat's point of view: *I try to make myself at home and then they unpredictably get all scary.*

A cat can only communicate with a fellow creature who they think would be capable of such communication. Likewise, humans who do not realize they can communicate with their cat will continue trying counter-productive training measures.

Then no one gets to the all important, so enjoyable, *spoiling*. Which is what actually leads to training.

Training is really about asking the cat for favors. To get them, we have to give them. Then the cat, compelled by the same Law of Reciprocity, will let us suggest the right places to scratch, good things to play with, and items that should be left alone.

I find swapping favors with my cats to be the training method which has the advantage of *actually working*, compared to other attempted cat training methods.

Consider my reader's cat when presented with a dilemma: "dining room table" is a no, but that "exact kind of box" is a yes. Since Cats are Lawyers I am not surprised that T– went for the box. T– knows he can explore boxes like this, and so he decided he can explore this one, no matter where it is. Or, at least, he can make a plausible case for acting on precedent that way.

T– was not being defiant or bad. I think the letter writer was correct in taking the blame for leaving a tempting box in the wrong place. This is what happened to us when Mr WayofCats left Father Christmas in the wrong place; a place that implied it was now open season on Father Christmas.

Finding T– on the dining room table would be another matter, but that is not what happened here. While I also understand my reader's wife thinking that he "lets T– get away with too much", her fears are actually groundless.

T– does not need to be controlled. That is a *fear of spoiling*; as though indulgence will imply we don't mean what we say about good behavior.

Indulgence is its own regulator

If we don't mind our cat doing something, we can happily let our cat do something.

If we don't want our cat to be somewhere, such as the dining room table or the kitchen counters, we let them know we would prefer they stay off that place, and they will listen.

There doesn't have to be any coercion, on either side. That is the beauty of it.

• Our cat will test the "limits of the law"

• Until we indicate we don't want to them to take things that far

• Which is when our cat will stop

The fact that we indulge them *creates the love* which will stop them from going too far. They listen to us *because* we spoil and indulge them. This is how we influence them and built our Bond of Trust.

We've shown, over and over, that we have their best interests at heart. So they actually want to listen to us, and do as they are requested.

Apologies and Gratitude

In a relationship full of feelings, there are going to be times when feelings are hurt. Since friendship is what this friendship is all about.

I often get presented with dilemmas like this:

> Creampuff was such an affectionate kitten. But then I had to give medicine/bath/something-they-hated and now they avoid me.
>
> My heart is broken.

It's bad enough when they come home grumpy from a vet visit. But sometimes, we are the ones who have to do something they hate. Then they act like they hate us for it. It's awful. But what we've got here is a failure to communicate.

What we are thinking is, *Don't they know I had to do that for their own good?*

Well, no. Obviously, they don't. Because their hearts are now broken. They thought we loved them.

This problem usually occurs early in the relationship, before we have established much trust. It's a special problem in rescue, when we have to look into a sad little face and say, *Hey, your troubles are over. Now let's treat those nasty injuries and illnesses.*

The lesson here is that we cannot take budding affection for granted. Too often, we relax and enjoy the easy companionship of a young kitten, or the quick gratitude of the rescued cat. We don't make special efforts because right now, we don't have to.

Then we have no reserves to draw upon when we have to perform an unpleasant task.

How to get it over with

We can head off trouble if we perform the function in a low stress manner. We can want to pounce on them and get it done. Even though we had to do it, too much muscle is not the best way to do it.

We can take steps which soothe hurt feelings; and keep them from feeling so rejected. I pick up tips from savvy vet techs; whatever I do, I do with a lot of verbal assurance, pauses for petting and soothing, and in a low-stress manner.

This communicates much more reassurance than us getting all crazed and anxious about doing it, holding them too hard, and making them feel threatened. Poor handling of this situation will give a cat the feeling that we are both Dr. Jekyll and Mr. Hyde.

• See page 209: Medicate a cat

Always make it up to them, right afterwards, and whenever they act distressed. If they like treats, great. Show them the treats before the procedure, and give it to them afterwards.

Now, there are mixed emotions about whatever it is... and some of them are good ones.

Apology Tour

We are sorry we had to do this, and we should show it.

• Lie on the floor and say how glad we are that is over so we can all be friends again.

• Chase them to wherever they are hiding and apologize, over and over.

• Show them a favorite toy and and get out the good catnip.

Whatever they love, let them know we will continue to give it to them.

It is never too late to apologize, Make a Fuss, and tell them we love them. Yes, it's true they used to come running up to us after work, and now they leave the room when we enter it. But that is because they worry we no longer love them.

We can fix that. Because our cat might be sending affectionate signals more than we realize. We should notice.

It was something I picked up early on. I would do something for my cat, and they would come around later to make some gesture that added up to, "Thanks." They loved it when I noticed that was what they were doing. I did it more. They did it more. It's a great feeling to both give and get.

I was missing a lot, at first, because I wasn't tuning my Cat Radio to pick up the subtler signs of cat affection. Cat enthusiasm is not measured by expended external energy, the way dog enthusiasm is. With cats, the smallest look or gesture is all the more powerful by its quietness.

• Cats use small signals to say big things.

Many of these affectionate gestures can be lost on the casual observer. Do we come in the room, and our "sleeping" cat opens their eyes enough to notice us? We've probably been given a Cat Kiss, and we should, in all politeness, return it. We might be familiar with the head butt when we put down the dish of food or clean the litter box, but there are many ways our cat shows affection and gratitude.

I come into the bedroom to grab something, and I say sweet things to the cats sleeping on the bed. If they move, I give them a head kiss.

Takes a second, but I have put a warm glow through a cat's body, the same way as their sending me an affection signal makes me feel a jolt of happiness. By not picking up all of our cat's signals, we could be missing out on affection.

I never want to miss out on that.

Gift of Empathy

It's easy for me to spoil my cats. Not only is this my personality default, I know they appreciate it. I rely on the fact that their emotions are intense and readily visible; once we know what to look for.

This also applies to our cats, whose sensitivity to body language means we humans are broadcasting like a radio station when it comes to our moods. This can seem like a bad thing when we don't understand why our cat is being so demanding and clingy all of a sudden.

- Can't they tell we are upset?

- Yes, they can.

- That is why they are trying to help out.

Paw of Compassion

Our cats can sense sadness, and wish to comfort us. But this is not the only emotion our cats can pick up. Our excitement, our apprehension, or our deep concentration on something can all create mirror-image emotions in our cats.

Sometimes the **Paw of Compassion** is literal, as when they lay their paw on our arm or leg. Sometimes it's a head rubbed across our cheek or forehead, sometimes it's curling up near us. But our cats do seem moved to comfort us when they know we are down.

Cats also have a human-compatible emotional range, with neurological, hormonal, and genetic systems which are far more alike than they are different. Grief has been observed in many wild species following the death of a mate, parent, offspring or pack-mate. Feline grief at the death of a long-term human or feline companion can include severe mental disturbance.

Here Tristan reaches for me to share an intimate moment.

I continue to think all mammals who live in a social structure tend to react in similar, and mutually understandable, ways.

Social network

Our cats are used to evaluating our behavior and seeing how it impacts their needs. There might be an element of selfishness in our cat's strong interest in our moods; but no more than it would be for our own children, partners, or friends who rely on our mutual assistance for physical or emotional needs.

I find that the more I interact with my cats, the more they develop their companionship skills. They are happiest when they contribute to our day to day routine. Nicely enough, this results in us being happy too, since we have a little someone who will notice our moods and try to be of service. They can clown or cuddle, depending on their personality and our needs.

Anyone with a close cat relationship has a story about how their cats gather around when they are sick or sad. Under such circumstances, it's undeniable that our cats are concerned about us.

It's the validation

We can help our cats feel better when we acknowledge their emotions. Our cats make us feel better when they do the same. I am always happy to be home from work, but an observer would not be able to see that my cats took much notice of my return, even when I greet them.

However, it takes only a short while for them to get up and come greet me wherever I am. Then I act thrilled to see them. This revs up their motors and they get even more excited. Within minutes, this builds into a rowdy game, and then a cuddling session on the couch.

If I come home and flop on the couch from a trying day, they pick up on the changed attitude. They peer over my recumbent body and ears flicker as they wonder why today is different. Is it them? No, it's not, and their amusing antics soon have me smiling, kissing heads, and feeling some good energy.

When we build a Bond of Trust between us and our cats, we use their sensitivity to both our advantage. The more our care meets their needs, the more time and motivation they have to pick up on our moods and try to take care of us. Then we can see the loving motives in their engagement antics.

We always feel comforted when another being "picks up" on our feelings and shares them with us. It's something that improves with practice.

Cats understand friendship

This makes everything else possible. Because friendship is our goal, we must respect our cat, and understand that this is a reciprocal relationship. When it comes to friendship, we are equals.

Neither of us is The Boss. We are equally invested in making each other happy. We do this because friendship is the only way we can get good behavior from our cat.

It's also the only way are cats are free to love us as much as they can.

That's our real goal.

Selection

We reach cats through their personality.

Cat Types help us choose the traits we want.

I was asked to bring home a kitten who was social, mellow, and could get what he needed in our small apartment.

I knew we needed a Beta Cat Type, and I knew how to spot them at almost any age. Reverend Jim turned out to be exactly the cat we needed.

Like his comedy namesake, he only needed a bit of help figuring out the world.

Their Types

Selection is about choices we didn't know we could make.

Many of us acquire a cat accidentally. A stray comes begging, a friend or relative has to rehome their cat, or we find an abandoned kitten. This is often how we come to cats — by not meaning to.

When we go to the shelter we often seek a kitten because we want to dodge a potential bad upbringing. We think we can "mold" the kitten into the kind of cat we want. We think there must be something wrong with the grown cats or they wouldn't have wound up in the shelter. We shun the senior cats because we don't think we'll have enough time with them.

Once we clear out our mental misconceptions about who cats are, and what they can do, we can go about the important task of *recognizing* and *developing* **Cat Potential**.

My experience in adopting Reverend Jim is a fine example of choosing mindfully. Because I recognized his dominant breed, I knew he was a Beta Cat Type. Now I knew this cat's skill set. I also had a better understanding of his problems, and how to fix them. All of these expectations were made with some confidence because I knew his Type.

There are three different Cat Types: **Alpha, Beta,** and **Gamma**. These types are distributed along a spectrum of personality.

In classic statistics distribution, most cats are Betas, and fall into the 2/3rds of the population in the middle. They can also be a mix along this continuum, with Betas leaning either Alpha or Gamma, and Alphas and Gammas themselves expressing their Type with varying strengths.

Cats are all unique personalities, but knowing their Cat Type lets us understand how this aspect of their personality influences interaction with their environment.

- Gammas *don't know they can* make any changes to their environment.

- Betas will *get us to make changes* to their environment.

- Alphas *go ahead and change* their environment.

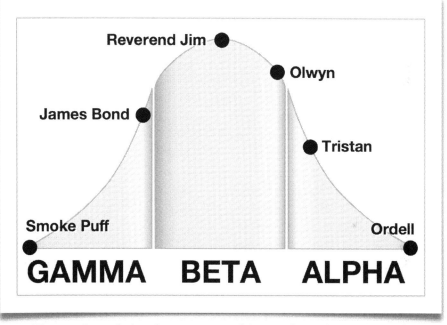

I have plotted six of my cats on this graph to show the wide distribution of this spectrum of traits.

Knowing what we're getting is so important to happy cat relationships. We wanted a cat who will quietly cuddle with us during a binge-watch of our favorite show, and instead we got someone who wants to climb the drapes and disassemble our favorite art object. Or maybe we wanted lots of play and interaction, and our cat only wants to find all the places in the home where they can do their Zen contemplation.

Choose wisely

The cat on the far right of the graph, the very Alpha Cat Type, Ordell, had to be rehomed because our tiny apartment could not contain him. The friend who agreed to foster him "until he calms down" had a two-story home where he could launch himself from the middle of the stairs, snag the curtain at the bottom, swing out into the middle of the living room, and land with a thud. That was what he needed.

She fell in love with him and we decided to let him go to a better home with her, so it all worked out. Because he was twelve years old before he even *started* to calm down.

Years later, we acquired Tristan as a foster kitten. By six weeks, when most cats start revealing their Cat Type, I realized he was leaning Alpha. Tristan has a lot of Siamese in him, including the verbal abilities and the kink at the end of his tail.

Fortunately for all of us, he turned out to be less so than Ordell. So, with cat trees and having more assertive cats to help keep him busy, we were able to meet his needs. And keep him.

If we have fallen in love, it might not matter what Cat Type they are, as long as we can provide what they require. That is the vital importance of choosing a cat mindfully.

• Does this cat meet our needs?

• Can we meet the needs of this cat?

At the other extreme on the left, with my rescued Smokepuff, we get emphasis on the Gamma's traits of close observation, ability to track tiny details, and heightened sensitivity to change. He was very Gamma Cat Type. He was easily upset by change, but also trusted his humans, and was able to be reassured. He liked studying things, even things that — to humans — weren't very interesting. He liked his affection low-key and with a soft voice.

Smokepuff was probably a backyard breeder version of the Chantilly-Tiffany; a cat with a lot of Persian in them.

Buddy with the Beta

Right in the middle is our total Beta Cat Type, Reverend Jim. He is our designated Kitten Wrangler, who loves to clean baby heads and show them the ropes. He is social with both humans and felines, he loves to cuddle, he loves playing with toy mice and feather toys. In appearance and temperament, he is classic Maine Coon Cat, though a mix.

James Bond (Norwegian Forest Cat mix) was a Beta who leaned Gamma, while Olwyn (Norwegian Forest Cat mix) is a Beta who leans Alpha. These two developed a lovely Mentor/Protege relationship.

The body construction of Beta Cat Type is a cat between the elongated shape of the Foreign Breeds (Alpha) and the solid, "cobby", build of the sturdy Persian (Gammas). While my distribution curve indicates two thirds of cats are Betas, we need to remember that many of them lean Alpha or Gamma, and can mix these traits.

• For many cats, their Type is a state of mind, not a body type.

Knowing the Cat Types lets us choose the kind of cat who would suit us best. We will also know our best strategies when it comes to caring for them, playing with them, and training them.

Cat Type Clues

As early as six weeks, kittens start showing the breed clues that indicate where they might land on the Cat Type spectrum. We can identify head and body characteristics, with distinctive ear and eye and paw shapes.

These are all useful clues to how they will express themselves, view their environment, and what they will expect from it. These are all clues about how they will express their *personality*.

Body types

People are often attracted to certain breeds because of their visual beauty. Nothing wrong with that, but we should make sure the personality behind that face and body will fit into our home.

The wild look of many Alpha Cat Types like the Abyssinian, or the beautiful "points" of the Siamese and Balinese breeds, should not be the only reason we want one. These cats are highly Foreign in their body types, being long and lean and energetic. Cat trees are a must, and often, cat exercise wheels, too.

Persians, Exotic Shorthairs, and Manx breeds have body types known as Cobby. Their shapes are the opposite, being sturdy and well-muscled, with large paws, deep chests, and broad heads. One thing to look for is what I call the "softball head" which it is large and round. They tend to mellow early, and hate to be a bother.

If they are long-haired, a trait that shows up early in kitten ears and paws, we can expect a Beta to Gamma kind of personality, because long hair is a Persian influence. As Gammas, they aren't going to complain until things have gotten out of hand. We must check in with them to keep that from happening.

Maine Coon Cats, Norwegian Forest Cats, and Siberians are all considered Northern breeds which are also natural breeds, with long fur that is interspersed with coarser "guard hairs" which make grooming them less frequent than the daily attention a more Persian coat requires.

Short-haired cats with sturdy bodies, like British and American Shorthairs, are likely Betas, but mixes are a delightful surprise package. That means we need to observe their activities as much as we do their physical traits.

We need to add up all the clues to get an accurate picture of what a particular kitten will become.

Tristan demonstrates the "paws-on" attitude of the Alpha Cat Type. His long legs and pointy paws were an early clue.

Male or female

It is notoriously difficult to figure out the sex of young kittens. Fortunately, it's rarely important to do so. Male or female has never been more than a blip on the radar screen of cat personalities, especially for responsible pet owners who spay or neuter.

As a tendency, males are more likely to be goofballs, while females, less so. If we get a tortoiseshell or calico, they are usually female and on the bossy side, because their tri-color coats reliably indicate a an XX chromosome and a strong-willed personality known as **Tortitude**.

To make an educated guess about a given kitten's assertiveness level requires a little more interaction. If the shelter or home that has kittens offers the option of spending some time alone with them, take it.

Bring some toys. If we slowly place the toy on the floor, what happens? (Do it slowly. Tossing it out will make almost any kitten chase it, out of sheer reflex.)

Do they take intervals to study it or immediately start batting it around? Do they watch it from a distance to see if it continues to move on its own?

The more cautious the kitten, the more likely they are to be a Gamma. The quicker they manipulate it, the more confident they are about manipulating their environment, and the more likely they lean Alpha.

A soft ring toy is helpful because it will sooner or later be grabbed in a way that makes it flip over and bop the kitten on the head. Gammas will back off. Betas will hesitate. Alphas will immediately renew the attack.

Does the kitten fix their attention on single objects, or keep looking for angles everywhere? The more they look around from all angles, the more Alpha they will be. Gammas find objects in the environment and study them fixedly, and will be more sensitive to change as a result.

The box test

Place the kitten in an empty cardboard box, too high to scramble out of easily.

• Gamma kittens will simply sit there for a while, pondering this development.

• Betas will start patrolling the sides, considering their options.

• Alphas will try to get out of the box.

All of these clues will tell us many things which will impact how we share affection, how quickly they will accept training suggestions, and even the kinds of toys they will like.

Cats not only express a broad range of genetics, kittens in a litter can have different fathers. A female in heat won't leave that state until her body signals that she is pregnant, and that can take long enough for her to have more than one encounter. So kittens in a litter can be any Type, and not much alike.

Gammas can attract people who are drawn to their shy qualities. However, we must be aware that this is not a shy cat who needs to come out of their shell. Caution and low-key devotion to their loved ones is going to stay a part of any Gamma cat.

• Gamma kittens crouch with more of a huddle, and often look at things close up.

• The Beta kitten often tries to make eye contact with us.

• The Alpha kitten often has their vision fixed on distance and darting around, like they are computing trajectories.

Heads with dome shapes are likely more Gamma, pointed faces more likely Alpha. If we can't decide, probably Beta. They blend all the traits.

Cat Type Comparison

As someone who has had all of these animals as pets, I can say:

The Beta is the dog cat

They use their social skills to ask us to manipulate our mutual environment. The key to happy Betas is giving them plenty of outlets to exercise their talents for friendship, routines, and organization. This lets them be their true selves; compassionate, highly-invested, community contributors.

Their forgiving nature smooths out grievances, even ones they were not involved in. Maybe not the life of the party, but definitely the soul of the house, Betas will work at everyone getting along. Their delight in any other friendly creature is infectious.

It is so easy to be friends with them and make them happy. Often, they are Greeter Cats. Betas are born with the most innate trust of humans.

Don't leave a Beta with high social needs without companionship. Some Betas will self-amuse and can handle being alone during the day, provided we give them plenty of social time when we are home. Since they get along with other cats so well, starting off with two Betas is the best way of covering their needs for interaction.

To find one, look for round heads and the body type known as medium, with neither the long slenderness of Alphas or the stocky big-boned builds of a Gamma. They have prominent facial structures, adaptable personalities, and a high interest in prey behavior.

Not only are they the most common Cat Type, interbreeding of any groups of cats tends to produce Betas, as the more extreme characteristics of the Alpha and Gamma types are moderated with Beta influence.

Domestic Shorthair is the core Beta heritage, and can appear in the most unlikely of places.

The Gamma is the rabbit cat

Their nature is to be sweet, trusting, and compliant. They rely on us to not only manipulate our mutual environment, but to monitor them about the status of their needs. They won't ask. They hate to be a bother.

The key to happy Gammas is *support*. If we can provide enough understanding, attention, and adoration for our Gammas, they will be devoted and delightful.

While they are the first to cultivate a mature demeanor as kittenhood progresses, they are also the most dependent Cat Type because of their aversion to getting into trouble. It can seem that Gammas are slow to grasp something, but that's not true. They have a slower thinking style. They "get it" but don't want to commit right away.

Gammas are also focused on our relationship, but in a low-key way. Gentle Gammas are easily provided for, yet require our small attentions more, than other Cat Types.

The cautions regarding Gammas start with their need for regular maintenance. Gammas tend to have long and fluffy fur, but good grooming practice is only the start. We cannot rely on them to let us know they are hungry or thirsty or are upset about something; *not quickly*. Gammas prefer to suffer in silence. We can't let that happen.

Of all cats, they are the most reliant on their schedules, and the least flexible with environmental stress or changes to their Cat Routines.

Look for the short nose, broadly set ears, thicker paws, and stocky bone structure that indicates Gamma traits. A wide-eyed expression, a quiet acceptance of the situation, and a close interest in details of their environment can point to Gamma mental traits in any cat.

Persians, and their combinations, are the core Gamma heritage.

GAMMA BETA ALPHA

(l to r) James Bond, Reverend Jim, Sir Tristan

The Alpha is the monkey cat

They combine ceaseless curiosity with an ease about manipulating our mutual environment. The key to happy Alphas is *enough*. If we can provide enough attention, play, and diversion for our Alphas, they will be amusing and delightful companions.

They are the cat who will be Forever Kitten in their outlook and energy levels. If we worry about "not enough play" and "they grow up too soon" we must consider an Alpha.

• If, that is, we feel ready.

• This is the most challenging Cat Type of them all.

It's not that Alphas misbehave on purpose. In the heat of their devotion to interesting activities, they can lose track of what they are supposed to do, or not do. When they express their love, it is as open and dramatic as everything else they do, which is how Alpha fans stay fans. Charm is one of their Superpowers.

This Cat Type offers endless fun. The status won't be quo for long with an Alpha investigating. Guests love the Alpha, and the Alpha loves them back. While not as available for stranger-petting as a Beta, they are the most likely cat type to appear and perform for guests. They love the spotlight.

We never wonder where we stand when an Alpha loves us; and loves us some more. Delightfully mischievous and highly opinionated, they require more management than other Cat Types.

We must remember that Alphas want what they want very much and they'd like it now. Mentally and physically, we absolutely must wear them out. Again.

Alphas tend to be long and lean, with long noses, large oval ears, and pointy paws. Often verbal, they are intense about whatever interests them.

Siamese is the core Alpha heritage, and all Foreign types express some Alpha traits.

Shelter vs Cat Breeder

• Should we get a purebred cat?

• Should we get a shelter cat?

• Should we rescue a purebred cat from the shelter?

• It depends.

I'm a huge fan of mixed breeds. But I'm not one to say "Never get a purebred," because *ethical* cat breeders tend to be devoted lovers of the particular traits that go into the different breeds. Without them, these traits wouldn't show up in the shelter for the rest of us to enjoy.

I want to caution that getting a purebred is about reliably acquiring certain traits from cat breeding.

• It is their predictability which is the value.

• We can work this problem from the other end and find a shelter cat with those traits.

• All we need to do is *look for those traits*.

Egyptian Mau is a very rare breed. Their traits are, per their online entry on the Cat Fanciers Association website:

• These cats display exceptional intelligence and exhibit a fierce loyalty to their owners. Even though domesticated, several characteristics of their early ancestors have been retained. These include the Cheetah gait and a loose skin flap that extends from flank to hind leg, which allows the Mau remarkable freedom and agility in twisting and jumping.

• Most people are attracted to Egyptian Mau because of their exotic good looks. They fall in love with them because of their incredible, irrepressible personalities. All cats are characters, but these, well, they're absolutely enchanting. Like all cats, they are individuals, one and all, but typical for the breed they tend to take it to extremes. Friendly to everyone in the family, they tend to be cautious with strangers and select their Special Person. On their own territory, they tend to be extremely outgoing with absolutely no fear and a ton of curiosity. They make wonderful companions.

• All true. And… *all Tristan.*

• I got Tristan from a nearby rural field after he'd been abandoned by his mother, a local cat of mixed heritage who had been earlier abandoned, unspayed and unready, to the outdoors. Father unknown, but highly unlikely to be some renegade Egyptian Mau; who could, in any case, donate only half of those genes to their offspring.

• Tristan is not a purebred Egyptian Mau; except he's got all those traits. So how did Tristan happen? The dice roll of genetics. In D&D terms, he rolled for Ancient Wisdom, and scored very high.

Look for what we want

• All the genes in all the cats exist in every cat. Otherwise, we couldn't tease out certain traits to build into the purebred cat of today. This means that these traits lurk everywhere, waiting for the right combinations to pop up in a recognizable way.

• The Siamese coat with points, the Maine Coon trill-voice, and the long hair of the Persian can be seen in lots of different shelters, especially in places where certain breeds have been popular. They have contributed more of those genes into the local pool.

A large number of cats, interbreeding, will wind up moderating their more extreme characteristics to reach an EveryCat; the Domestic Shorthair.

Even purebred cats can be born with different degrees of the different traits. Much more than dog breeders, cat breeders have to do things like mate Manxes of varying degrees of tail-lessness to get healthy Manxes.

Without even trying I've had all kinds of cat breeds. Why settle for one when we can have two or three in one cat?

Purebreds can't be a bargain

However, I must emphasize *ethical* cat breeder. That means they care about breeding the healthiest cats they can, have their breeding cats be household pets as much as possible, and take excellent care of everyone.

They will not breed to fashion, like the terrible practice of Persians with faces so flat they have trouble eating and breathing. It means managing tricky genetics so they don't have inbred cats with too much of a particular trait or with inherited disease. It means not being a backyard breeder with no concern for veterinary care or the quality of the kittens they are selling.

That is why their kittens are expensive. That is why you should not get a "purebred bargain" unless prepared for a demanding socialization challenge or a heartbreaking genetic issue. People think that having a pedigreed cat implies some kind of quality, as thought a purebred is somehow better than a mixed breed. But that is not what it means.

• A purebred is a recognized breed whose parents were both recognized breeds. And that's it.

• That's all it means.

Choose the cat, not the label

We do not need to feel a cat is a "black box" of unknowns. We think about the kind of cat we want, we decide on the traits which would suit us best, then we look for the cat who displays those traits.

Tristan's distinctive markings include stripes, spots, and "ticking" which is the white tips of his hair, seen on his back.

If our prospective cat tries to connect with us; with their paw, with their eyes, and with their voice; then they are showing themselves to be willing to meet us halfway. This vital social connection between two beings is all we need to get started.

• Recognizing this connection is the key to choosing the right shelter cat.

Every cat in a shelter has a problem. But most of the time, it's something quite easily fixed. **They don't have a home.**

If the cat who appeals to us *appeals to us*... then their problem is that they aren't getting enough love.

We can fix that, can't we?

The Mold-a-Cat Myth

Often, people will choose a kitten because they think they can "mold" them into the cat they want to have. They can cloak their uncertainty about which cat to choose by picking an age they think they can influence.

- It's wonderful to raise a kitten.

- It's a mistake to think we can "mold" them into a particular cat.

From her kittenhood to peak of adulthood, Olwyn has always been affectionate, strong-minded, and fond of Supervising.

While body types can vary along the Cat Type distribution curve, the expression of a Cat Type personality stays consistent. A high energy Alpha kitten will not mellow with age and become a laidback Beta window watcher. A shy cat might be Gamma, or might need to recover from the trauma of abandonment.

We always need to consider the whole cat. At any point in their lifespan, they are half nature, and half nurture.

So we can't skip the Choosing step by getting a kitten. Or we can wind up with a cat with traits we didn't expect, because kittens don't have their Types as readily seen, or display their full set of traits, the way an adult cat does. Personalities tend to be indelible, whether it is a cat or a human.

We can maximize Cat Potential, but we cannot change their essential nature.

I knew Olwyn was going to have Tortitude because of her tortoiseshell pattern. I didn't know the strength it would be, but I knew she would never be mellow, like RJ.

Pros and cons

Anyone who is contemplating a kitten should also be familiar with their possible disadvantages. Kittens are easy sells and there's nothing wrong with adopting them. It is still a good idea to understand appropriate age choosing, from all angles. Because there's equal amounts of enjoyment in adopting a teen, adult, or senior cat.

The cuteness is in negative correlation with their thinking skills. The younger the kitten, the more air-headed they are. Maturation also varies in speed by Cat Type. Gammas act more mature, more quickly, while we can be "reminding" a seemingly heedless Alpha for months to come.

Many potential cat adopters are apprehensive about getting a cat who is already "fully baked". *What if they learned all the wrong things?* But this exaggerates our influence upon our kitten. Our greatest impact upon either kitten or cat is how they *feel about us*. That has no age or Cat Type barrier.

Kittens must grow into understanding how humans work, and how to give each other the benefit of the doubt when we hurt each other's feelings. Adult cats come with this understanding already in place. This is how we grow a strong and enduring relationship.

It can come from the tiniest, and most adorable, of seeds; or it can come from a sturdy oak.

We also need to adjust our concept of "kitten". There's actually a big window where we can enjoy a young cat during their growing up stage. Cats don't mature for at least three years. The big kittens, from Persian or Northern breed lines, take even longer.

- That means any cat, under three, is *not grown up* yet.

- It doesn't matter how *big* they are.

- It's about how *mature* they are.

If they have been rushed along that path too soon, a good home will let them slow down and catch up.

If they are feeling secure and cared for, they can keep, or rediscover, their baby behaviors. They can take their time growing up. If the process has been interrupted, the young cat will catch up on parts of their kittenhood they missed, in much the same way their bodies can catch up and get over past malnutrition.

All a work in progress

Likewise, one of my favorite parts is taking on a cat of uncertain age and letting them bloom into the cat they should have been all along. Their minds develop and that lush fur, bright eyes, and happy confidence will make them seem younger. This transformation is thrilling and brings us closer, even if we didn't know them from birth.

When it comes to choosing, the clearest cat to "read" is actually the adult cat. They have revealed all of their physical potential, they have developed their brain and communication skills, they have loved and lost.

• They have been there and done that… and are willing to do it again.

From years of rescue, I can confidently state that it is truly rare to be unpleasantly surprised by hidden flaws in such an adoption. Older cats are less meltingly cute, but they are also less exasperating. They have acquired self-discipline, learn more quickly, and have a few tricks of their own they would like to teach us.

The difference between bringing home a kitten or adult cat is mostly that of time frame. For a kitten, there will be some moving of them from couch to scratching post. For an adult, we see them eyeing the couch, and we helpfully show them that the scratching post is better. In both cases, we see them using their scratching post, and we praise them and show affection.

Kittens need reminding for months. Adult cats learn the ropes within a week or two. And we all wind up in the same place. We don't need to "start from scratch" with our cat to get a good result.

• This gives us flexibility in choosing.

• We can concentrate on *Who They Are.*

• Not *How Old They Are.*

Raising a kitten and making friends with an older cat differs only in the details. Both explore their new space, test our boundaries and communication skills, and can only move at the speed of their *trust.*

At all ages, we supply loving guidance, not fear and punishment.

Choosing Shelter Cats

I say it all the time: Don't fear the shelter cat.

Many people think the shelter is full of other people's problem cats. They can't imagine giving up a beloved cat for anything less than a dire, uncontrollable, issue. I only wish everyone felt that way.

The cats in the shelter do have a terrible problem. They were given up by the people who regard them as things to be owned, not friends to be loved.

There's not a thing wrong with the cat in question, except they don't have a home. Someone passed away, someone moved and dumped them, someone had a child or took up a new hobby or got rid of the growing, no-longer-so-cute kitten by throwing them out and ignoring them.

- Cats suffer with *owner problems*

- Which won't be *friend problems*

Suffering and neglected cats can misbehave in a misguided attempt to signal their distress, but cat owners don't know how to communicate. They take actions which only worsen the stress.

A bright cat, easily bored, can seem overactive because they are starved for stimulus. A naturally energetic cat can be penalized when they start getting bigger and their tendency to knock things over is not cute anymore. A cat starved for affection can wail all night, scratch or play with the wrong things, miss their litter box, or otherwise show signs of stress.

Ironically, these are the cats who bloom in the shelter. So many times shelter workers will exclaim over anyone passing up such a gem of a cat.

• They were cats with problems only because of *how they were treated.*

• Once given affection and support, they are no longer cats with problems.

Adorable, but at this age Tristan needed care around the clock.

There's all kinds of misconceptions about "used cats", but the rise of enlightened cat shelters has helped greatly to calm these fears. Instead of a scared cat in a cage with the clock ticking down, they are cats who are behaving much more closely to their true nature, and so, able to show off their true nature.

For your consideration

There are two more variations on cat age, which are the opposite ends of the range.

—*Senior cats* are not only for senior people, though they do work out wonderfully. They will play, though it tends to take the form of attacking from ambush at the perfect time instead of headlong scampering across the room. But once they start getting into double digits in age, senior cats express themselves in mental powers, not physical ones.

The biggest worry with senior cats is possible health problems from aging, but this cat must have gotten good care or they wouldn't be here today. This often happens to beloved cats who suffered the death of their person, and that person's relatives consider them disposable.

They can easily have half their lifetime still ahead of them, and a wonderful capacity for love is still there. The way I see it is that we get to appreciate this peak of cat powers without having to wait while it develops.

—*Teen cats* are an unsung delight. Midway between baby and adult, they have elements of both. They can be as goofy and playful as kittens, with the advantage of better thinking skills and an actual attention span.

Finding one of these leggy, big-eared, treasures in a shelter means we have to remember they can be mistaken for an adult, yet still need all the care and cultivation of a younger kitten. We're only missing a few months of their kittenhood, after all. The whole rest of the cat is still ours to enjoy.

At any of these stages beyond kitten, we connect with a cat who offers more visible clues to their Cat Potential. Breed traits are fully recognizable, their energies are on display, their curiosity and caution is more visible. We can interact at a deeper and more revealing level than we can with kittens, and feel more confident of the feedback we get.

Cats are constantly developing

It would be a lonely world if we were restricted to only friends we had made by kindergarten age. Remember how easy it was to make friends back then? *We live next to each other. We have Barbies. I like trucks.*

All too often, such friends fall away as we develop more mature and personalized interests, and find our old friends do not share them. We grow apart, which is often sad, but the important thing is, we grow.

So it is with cats.

When we meet friends as adults, we discover shared interests. We listen to the stories of their lives. There is drama and heartbreak and celebrations. It's fascinating.

Adopting an adult cat reminds me of how we sit down for a movie to meet an interesting character in the middle of a crisis. Along the way, we learn a lot about them, root for them, and share in how they cope with challenges.

• This is who the shelter cat is.

• A fascinating being at a crossroads.

We can join them, and make it into a shared journey.

Bridge to Adults

It might astonish us to discover how swiftly an already grown cat can adapt to our requests and trigger a flood of mutual love and understanding, It is far faster than getting a kitten to think before they act.

- It's all a matter of choosing the "perfect stranger".

To build a bridge to grown cats, we should expect some exploration, both of the house and ourselves. The older and wiser the cat, the more low key and reserved their first moves will be. A teen cat will tend to have bursts of frantic activity, which will be as emotional, only expressed in a different way. They will be open to friendship, but we shouldn't push for instant lap sitting or hugging.

They are still figuring us out. Let them proceed at their own pace. It's not a drawback that adult cats have already formed attitudes and strategies. That's where the fun comes in.

At any age that they join our household, the early stage is when they are still figuring us out, and we should let them proceed at their own pace.

Gift them

We should always give them a Security Object of their own, and make a fuss over the presentation.

Consider a little pillow, small stuffed animal, or any fabric object which can be given to them as a gift. Rub the object on the back of our neck, to pick up our scent, before giving it to them.

Make a point of putting it in a spot they have already shown an interest in.

  • Any time we want to start engaging, we can use the object to focus their attention and signal our interest.

We should give them a tour of the house, talking up things that affect them. We should always take advantage of the mature cat's abilities. They can communicate, and understand our efforts, much more easily than younger cats.

Show them their bowls and their litter, of course, but also show them a window that has interesting views and the corner of the couch where you've already draped a throw to make it softer.

Even if the cat isn't good at understanding our words yet, they will always appreciate a happy tone and open-hearted effort. This is how we will show our desire for them to be comfortable and happy.

If the cat is not inclined to follow us around during the tour, do it anyway. Their hearing is good enough that they don't have to be in the room to hear our words. This will signal them that this is a room worth exploring later, on their own.

This routine, which we can repeat to reassure our new cat, will help them start to put together our words and our actions.

Meshing with us

When we perform our own routines, we should announce what we are doing, and point out where our cat can become a part of them.

Try to make playtime, dinnertime, and bedtime clear and recognizable events by signaling them beforehand, and not allowing these routines to be disrupted too often.

Most likely, our new adult cat has come to us from some kind of complete collapse of their previous life, no matter its quality, or lack of it, at the time. We need to make a special effort to acknowledge, and soothe, any anxieties they might have over the shape their new life will take.

Taking these steps to reassure the cat sends another, highly important, signal.

• It doesn't merely show we *care* about them.

• It shows we know *how* to care about them.

They will then relax into their new home more quickly. Only with calm and confidence can they start their most important work, which is seeing how much they can trust, and fall in love, with us.

They game us back

Getting "gamed" for the first time by a savvy adult cat is a moment of wonderment.

• Maybe we stumble into the dim bathroom for an after midnight pit stop, and discover they are waiting there for us.

• Maybe they are lying on our car keys in the morning, so we have to talk to them and pet them before we can get our keys back.

• Maybe they hid a shoe so we have to get down on the floor to look for it… and there's their face peeking out at us from under the bed.

The adult cat will tend to create moments where we can "discover" them. This is how they gauge our sincerity. Are we thrilled to see them? Do we appreciate the effort they have made? Are we sensitive enough to understand they can't risk overt gestures, not quite yet?

I know the fun begins as soon as our new cat, of whatever stage of growth and development, comes home. But I also feel that the fun need never stop, and indeed, grows, along with our cat.

Kitten is only the beginning of our cat, and when they are happy, we can see that kitten in them.

If we act suitably flattered, happy, and welcoming, we will encourage our new cat towards their own realization that we are, after all, worthy. The first time our new cat melts into our hand or lap, with adoring eyes and a full-throated purr, that's exactly how we will feel.

Cat Poker

I call this Cat Poker because we show each other our cards. So to speak.

We serve food, and our cat responds with an affectionate bump on our shin. We offer a toy, and our cat shows willingness to leave a knickknack alone, because now they have something better to play with. We settle in the living room, and our cat appears, wanting some lap time.

Let's play poker

This is all about love, and all about "seeing and raising" each other's loving gestures. When we respond to a cat's friendship gesture with one of our own, and the best part is that everyone wins.

As cats enter their adolescence, we might notice that the heedless affection of the kitten years is fading. People can become baffled and hurt by the growing kitten's displays of independence. They might not understand that their kitten is *signaling a progression* in the relationship.

They are becoming equal players, so the relationship develops into *taking turns* to show affection.

Whose turn is it?

When our cat acts indifferent, it is a game. They are hoping we will miss them, realize that we care about them, and then feel compelled to seek them out.

So that is what we must do.

As they grow up, their heart gets bigger. Tristan was able to slow down and think more.

If we miss the cat, *miss the cat*. Wander around, calling them, wondering aloud where they might be. Say how much we love them. Act happy when we do see them.

The concept of Make a Fuss is central here.

• It is important to fuss over the cat.

• So the cat will fuss over us.

What do I mean? It's simple: *Make a fuss over the cat*.

This is the greatest pitfall for those new to cats. They cluelessly wait for the cat to fuss over *them*, not realizing that the cat is likewise waiting.

Cat Poker is an essential skill in rescue. We might need to win over a cat who has experienced neglect of some kind. They fell for an offer of friendship before, and wound up betrayed and abandoned. Showing the cat that we are trustworthy means putting our own heart on the line when we ask for theirs.

Presence

- They regard *their* presence as a gift.

- They regard *our* presence as a gift.

- Cats give points for *showing up*.

A cat being near us is the same as a human speaking words of trust and affection. When we understand how **Presence** works for cats, we can make it work for us, too.

Since cats are so aware of their Giant Sensory Map, they are highly aware of all the other beings in the environment. That is how they enjoy taking a nap in the room we are in. All we have to do is look up and say their name occasionally, and they are happy to be noticed. We should feel happy they chose this room for their nap.

Some people find themselves wondering what they can do to have a more affectionate cat. Have they missed the boat?

No. There's always another boat coming in. We simply have to recognize it as such.

We might not realize, even as we make friendship gestures, that we might not be leaving a space for the cat to make friendship gestures of their own. At the time, sure. We extend a hand, they put a body part into it; so far, so good.

If we ask ourselves, "When does the cat make the first move?" and our answer is, "Not often," we have the basis for the myth that cats do not initiate affection.

But they do, of course they do. It's simply not recognized. Because the next move in Cat Poker can often be so subtle, it's not seen by the human. When not seen, it's not responded to. When not responded to, it makes the cat feel ignored. Then the relationship stays stuck.

We might have a cat who is overwhelmed by our attempts to make a big bold gesture, and we don't make the small ones they are seeking. This turns out to have a simple solution.

• If we *notice the cat* every time we notice the cat

Meet their eyes and give a quick blink. That's a Cat Kiss, and it says we want to be friends the way an extended hand to another human signals our good intentions. If we are seeing the cat, that's on purpose. They want to be acknowledged. Break out our Look of Delight.

Once we start seeking them out to perform these Affection Moves, they will show up more often. In these small steps, we can forge a new connection, or rebuild a shaky one.

• For cats, an emotional connection is *everything*

The essence of playing Cat Poker is to always be seeing and raising each other's cards.

The Power of Names

It is an important decision which might take only a moment and then influences a lifetime. It is choosing the name of our cat.

They need something special. Show some imagination. Choose something we will enjoy saying over and over again.

It's important to start with a great name. Not only will it be the basis for many affectionate nicknames to come, it is an early act that will inevitably reflect how we feel about the cat, and influence how the cat will then respond to us.

Not bothering to come up with a special name communicates a lack of interest, and also a lack of recognition of the uniqueness of each individual, whether human or feline.

Cats are, above all, individuals, and giving them a careless name does communicate a level of disinterest. We should give the new arrival a little observation, a little understanding, and a little acknowledgment.

What we feel when we say their name

For instance, if the name is blatantly one sex and the cat turns out to be the other, this need not matter. It certainly doesn't make any difference to our cat.

However, if we have some hesitancy in our voice, if the discrepancy is going to bother us, the name should be changed to a new variation. Whether we feel it is awkward to correct visitors about the sex of a cat or we are the one bothered with the cognitive dissonance, and sending a wrong signal to our cat with their own name.

Then our own sense of unease will be in our voice when we use that name. It will not seem as affectionate to use their name. We should not make their name into a source of vocal stress.

Stress that our cat will pick up on with their sensitive hearing, and then feel unloved.

- We should always pick a name that makes us feel excited, and interested, and happy.

- When we say our cat's name, it will make them feel excited, and interested, and happy.

The connection between our cat's name and our use of that name is important, because our cat is so exquisitely sensitive to our voice tones.

I send my cats messages with the emotional undertone in my voice. If they are being cooperative and scratching on their scratching post, I trill their name in happy tones, and they scratch all the harder from joy. It's excellent feedback that will encourage them to scratch where it is best for them to do so.

Training is communication

It about about telling our cats what we would like them to do. What motivates our cats to comply is the depth and strength of our relationship. Our respect and affection for each other is *what makes the magic happen.*

It starts with their name, and how we use their name. When we call our cats different names at different times, we are telling our cat how they seem to us at the moment.

If we feel warmly affectionate, we use baby talk and names that fit this mode of communication. If we are explaining a turn of events, we are more formal, to indicate we are conveying important information.

More the merrier

I use the most common version of Reverend Jim's name, RJ, for when I'm sitting on the couch typing away and Reverend Jim is walking across the room on some mission or other. But I can call his name, make eye contact, exchange Cat Kisses, and we both go back to our projects. I could have said anything to get Reverend Jim to make eye contact; but by using his name, I let him know *I noticed him on purpose.*

With longer or sillier names, I convey closeness. When I call Reverend Jim the *Big Ol' Puddin' of Love* I am using a long and elaborate version of his name to let him know I enjoy the way he settles his front paws and head on my lap to show affection. Puddin' is one of Reverend Jim's Qualifier Nouns; anything with that word in it refers to him.

Words have more meaning to humans than to cats. What cats listen for are the emotions in our voice.

Names are everywhere

Cats have so many names because there are so many ways to enjoy our cat. So what are my tips for naming, and nicknaming, our cat?

One way is to *wait for it.* The official name should come along once we feel we know their unique personality. Sometimes this comes quickly, but if it doesn't, a nickname will work perfectly well. After all, they'll need those, too.

If our cat is a kitten, they need a goofy kitten name, which we can use for their whole lives. If we didn't get them as a kitten, *give them a kitten name anyway.*

If we acquire the cat as an adult, they usually come with a name; which we can feel free to adjust or discard as we get to know them better.

• Cats learn all their names.

Name them so we can *say it with feeling.*

It's something I can't overstate. More than any other pet, cats very much care what we call them. And what it sounds like when they hear our voice say it.

Their name is a power we must always use for good.

Their Origin Story

Every cat starts with a story. The *how we got them* story. The day we went to the shelter, the stray who came to stay, the kitten from the parking lot. We tell these stories to our friends. We should tell them to our cats.

We can't tell the story without love in our voice. Cats respond to that. Putting emotion in our voice creates a tonal language, something that can be "read" by our cat.

Cats are emotionally driven creatures. They do not lie around planning their day coolly and rationally. They lie around thinking about feelings they like. To get them, they think about when and where they should show up to get that feeling.

So they will always be swayed by an emotional appeal. Telling them **Their Origin Story** is a lovely ritual which means we always have something sweet to tell the cat when we want a moment with them. The more we tell it, the more it becomes familiar and beloved.

A cat's story, told and retold, is something we create that will bind the two of us together, keeping the connection with that thrilling day we first met.

Remember?

The process of new cat selection is an expression of our hopes and dreams, but this can only be as expansive as our imagination allows. If we allow our own cat prejudices to cloud our minds about what is possible, we will not see what is right in front of us.

I write a great deal about Choosing because I feel it is a vitally important element of successful Cat Appreciation, yet one that the majority of cat advice outlets vastly ignores. Understanding what we are seeing in a potential cat or kitten will cut down on unwelcome surprises later. At the same time, I must acknowledge the importance of letting our heart do some choosing of its own.

The vibes

The heart is an equally important element of successful cat choosing. We can survey any number of worthy cat prospects, but often the choice comes down to **Feeling the Connection**.

RJ and his kitten Mithrandir are both Maine Coon Cat mixes, with rough beginnings that turned into happy endings.

There's something magical about seeing a kitten or cat and sensing the tug of some incipient bond. We might feel we have to give everybody a chance; we dutifully read the cage tags and speculate about what they might mean for us. Yet, we can find ourselves drawn back to that one fascinating face. It can make us feel a cat is meant to be.

This is where honesty about our own motives and abilities can help us avoid breaking both the hearts in question. A cat taken to a home where they cannot fit in is a cat who could have been taken by a more suitable person and placed in a more secure home. Choosing poorly might mean the struggle of trying to change a cat or trying to change our situation, and feeling terrible about the futility involved.

I would love to see more people understanding that kitten is not the only age of possible cat. Those who have already discovered the joys of acquiring cats at every age have begun to appear, but what is missing is often the element of deliberation. They come into people's lives as strays or fosters. If we decide we will be open to *what feeling comes to us*, this can be, literally, the best way to get our next cat.

Once we know the thrill of a cat who places a gentle paw on our arm, gazes into our eyes, and seeks a connection, we have the answer to the most important question of cat relationships.

- If we can *connect* with this cat, we can communicate with this cat.

- If we can *communicate* with this cat, we can *love* this cat.

All else flows.

Care

We reach cats through their instincts.

A cat's wants are a cat's needs.

Reverend Jim had to be nursed back to health slowly and carefully. We caught him up on all the nutrition he had missed and treated the infections which had developed.

He had lost so much fur he didn't look like the long-haired cat he was supposed to be. We taught him to enjoy grooming as his adult coat was finally able to show itself. We were starting to see the cat he should have been, all along.

Their Instincts

In some ways, cats are highly adaptive. They have switched from a wild environment to being comfortable in our home. They can subvert their predator behaviors into playing with toys and eating the contents of cans.

Under the influence of hormones and environmental stress, they will aggressively defend their hunting territory and live as loners. Without such compromising pressures, they are delightfully interactive and display amazing social skills.

Tristan stays on top of things.

Despite such flexibility, there are ways they are locked into their instincts. When it comes to using their litter box, they have certain rules their brains urge them to follow. The need to keep their claws and bodies in trim requires things to scratch that meet certain criteria. If they want to survey a room from a high vantage point, or hang out in a window with interesting views, they will be insistent about doing so.

Work with them, not against them

When we work with their instincts to get their needs met, our cats become relaxed and cooperative, happy and affectionate. If we struggle to get our cat to do something, it's usually a signal that this is an action their instincts are not comfortable with.

• Cat care problems are about not matching the cat's survival instincts.

Because cats are the least domesticated of all domestic animals. Archeological evidence keeps pushing back the date when cats began living with humans; it is currently estimated at between 12,000 and 15,000 years ago. It's not that long a time period when we consider evidence of dogs joining up with humans have estimates ranging from 15,000 to more than 100,000 years ago.

Dogs have distinct advantages when it comes to adapting to human needs. They are natural pack animals, used to power structures and doing what a pack leader asks of them. The dog's genome seems to be highly adjustable; scaling up to Great Danes and down to Chihuahuas.

While cats were deliberately not shaped to human preferences. They were "hired" as vermin eliminators, and it would have been foolhardy to adjust their genes to endanger their incredible skills in that area.

Cats are themselves. They have not changed to adapt to us all that much. Except, and this is key: over that time period, humans kept choosing the friendliest, cuddliest, and most tractable of the kittens in each litter.

So we can reach the cat's heart. We do so by letting them know we are their friends, because we are taking care of them in the ways they require.

The major adjustment many people must make when it comes to enjoying a great cat relationship is that, unlike any other pet arrangement, cat/human affection is based on *equality*.

The cat must be acknowledged as the one who knows the most about what makes them happy. They have insights we lack into their own care and desires. We will consult this acknowledged expert, and gain a devoted friend.

Or we can cling to our ego, our myths, our prejudices; and get into a battle of wills with the cat about how to address their needs. Previous experiences with dogs is completely misleading in this case.

Cats are not dogs

When we apply what I call the **Dog Template** to our cat relationship, we become frustrated, our cat becomes puzzled and frightened, and no one is happy and content.

Cats arrive already housebroken; what we want is for them to teach us how they need to have their litter cared for. A dog is happy with a mud puddle, while a cat has to be fussy about their water's cleanliness and freshness.

Dogs are omnivores, both hunters and scavengers, and notably not picky. Cats are obligate carnivores, with rigid rules about what they can, and cannot, eat.

I could make an endless list of how cats differ from dogs, but I don't have to. Human toddlers have the essentials when they point to different animals and say "Doggie" and "Kitty". If a two-year-old can tell the difference, the rest of us have no excuse at all.

We want to make the cat happy about their arrangements. In the wild, cats would spend a great deal of their time keeping track of their hunting territory and discovering, or creating, places for various life-saving activities. We need to match the important parts of those instincts so our cats are comfortable expressing them.

When we show our cat we listen to them about what makes them comfortable, that we care that they are happy, that their wants are fully as important as our own: then we will reap the benefits of doing it right. There are vast reserves of love and great varieties of interaction which cats can bring to the table.

Our cat's instincts are still as fresh and vital as they always were. So our cats can't help being stubborn about what their brain tells them is important to their survival. There's no negotiating with anyone's survival instincts.

• When we try to *ignore* what the cat wants because of their instincts, a cat can be an exasperating, even difficult, pet.

• When we *work with* our cat, it can be the easiest pet experience of all.

The Instruction Manual

We got our cat Tristan when he was three weeks old. He was found in a remote field, an abandoned kitten we had to feed and clean every two hours, the same way a mother cat would do. Mr WayofCats soon said, "Oh, now I understand why you call this the 'furry slug' stage."

Because we had to put his food into his mouth for him. His eyes couldn't focus. He was a wobbly walker at the best of times, but especially so when his belly got round from a feeding and

Baby Tristan dutifully cleaning the glop from his plate.

barely let his stubby legs reach beneath him. He needed cleaning, fore and aft, with a damp cloth, as he couldn't even go to the bathroom without gentle encouragement from a cotton ball on his behind.

Though it didn't seem that way when we were setting our alarm for every two hours, this stage didn't last very long. At four weeks and a bit, he was motoring all over the house. He could scamper around, feed himself, and use his little litter box. He could clean the areas he could reach. He was communicating with the other living beings in the home.

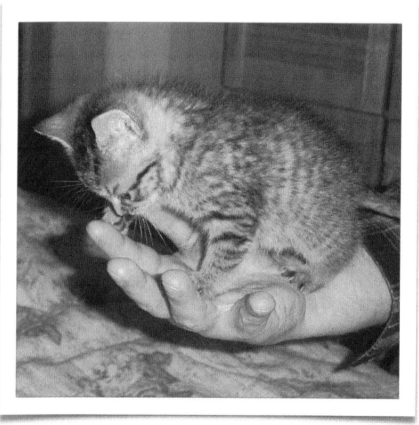

Baby Tristan, five weeks old and ready for action, though still too young to leave his mother.

He didn't have to *learn* any of these things. He was already running on instinct.

This example illustrates the cat's Built-in **Instruction Manual**. Very early in his life, Tristan was able to meet his own basic care needs. We humans provided the proper materials, correctly set up, and he was able to do a lot of his own maintenance.

Likewise, "training the cat" is mostly setting up the right things in the right places so our cats can take care of themselves. As they prefer. This well-known independence is actually a great advantage for us, too.

We don't have to puzzle out what the cat wants. They are happy to tell us. Each cat comes with their own Instruction Manual. The only thing we need to learn is: *how to listen.*

Everything is communication

Nothing good happens without information flowing between us and our cat. This is the core of the Bond of Trust we are building with our cat friend. It doesn't matter what the age of the cat is when we first meet.

We humans place these first, loving, foundation blocks by demonstrating that we know what they would like. We will respect their wishes regarding their food, water, bathroom, and sleeping needs. We are also willing to change what we provide if there's something wrong with it.

Whenever I am dealing with puzzling cat behavior, I remind myself that trying to work against a cat's instincts will always be doomed to failure. Their instincts are non-negotiable. This is about survival to them, which is why they are so stubborn and fussy. If we are honest, we can admit that humans are the same way.

Our feet in their paws

Imagine we come to a friend's house for an overnight visit. When they show us where we will sleep, it is a small, empty, closet. No matter how much our friend exclaims over how quiet, private, and clean this space is, we want to express our reservations. The floor space is too small to lie down to sleep, and we are without so much as a blanket to keep us warm or cushion us against the hard floor.

Our friend has provided only half of good human sleep requirements. If they argue with us about the half they are not providing, we feel they don't care about our sleep needs. *Why aren't they listening to us?* It makes us feel they do not respect our own understanding of what we need to be comfortable. It makes us feel they are not really our friends.

This is exactly the way our cat feels when we get upset about the cat rejecting our care gestures or not complying with our behavior demands.

"Why don't they like that food? What is wrong with their cat bed? When will they leave the couch alone?"

The answers are right under our nose all along. Usually in the form of the cat patiently trying to explain we have it only half right, and they will be glad to help us fix it.

- If our cat is *bothering* us

- It is because something is *bothering* our cat

Trying to tell us

People might find themselves unprepared for the close scrutiny, vocal instructions, and sheer amount and intensity of eye to eye staring which cats do. This is part of the cat's communication process, their Catspeak.

To some extent, we will need to mimic these things to communicate with the cat. Interacting with the cat, and imitating each other, are important early steps in this communication process.

In turn, our cat is studying us to interpret our body language, imitating our use of speech, and studying our faces to help them learn intentions.

That's why I say *cats are so easy*. If we listen to the cat, we can't mess up.

They will issue clear instructions most of the time. We don't even have to look anything up in their internal, constantly updated, Instruction Manual. They will gladly find the right page and constantly indicate the relevant bullet point until we get it.

Once we recognize that the "cat bothering us" is *how it all works.*

Litter Box Problems

Number one worst cat problem ever. Not that it makes anyone feel any better knowing that. In fact, this is one of those things we might not even tell our best friend. Or, worse, we suspect our best friend already knows.

Litter box problems can be solved. We should approach this calmly because we can act immediately to reduce the scope of the problem.

—*What to Do Right Away:* Isolate the cat in a room with food, water, and a litter box.

Don't have any clean litter handy? (There's your problem.) Clean the box as best you can. A bit of clean litter in a cardboard box is better than a whole box of dirty litter.

If we don't have an extra room, we can use the bathroom, which is designed for easy cleanup. This not only creates a space for us to feel some calm about finding accidents around the house, it will gives us vital clues about their behavior that we will use later, as we fix the litter arrangements that are causing the problems.

Often, what happens is that the cat gives us our first clue by happily using the clean litter in this nice, quiet, room. This can frustrate us all the more as we wonder why they are behaving now, and not before. We should calm down and realize we don't have a "broken" cat. We have a "broken" litter arrangement.

• See page 187: Is the litter box clean? Why clean is vital.

What if the cat doesn't use the nice clean litter in the quiet little room? Chances are, this is a cat signaling that they have a medical issue.

• See page 183: Is the cat sick? Why we must schedule a vet visit.

Unless there is a simple, yet too common, reason for all this trouble.

• See page 179: Has the cat been altered? Still need a vet visit.

Now we have reduced the places the cat can misbehave in, and we have reduced our own stress over finding these places. We can find and clean up all the potential problem areas, and think about what they might be telling us about what the cat needs.

Naturally, we will want to eliminate reminders around the house. We don't want them around, and we don't want them to remind the cat, either.

• See page 208: Clean Up After the Cat for more about getting rid of these reminders.

Discipline with litter box mistakes

We must also resolve to handle these situations differently in the future. Since what we were doing before *hadn't worked*, it shouldn't be difficult for us to give up this approach and substitute a new one.

We often have an immediate wrong reaction that will make the problem worse. *Don't* yell at the cat, *don't* drag them to where they messed up, and *don't* rub their noses in it. If we do these things with a cat, they will completely misinterpret what we are trying to tell them.

• It never works.

• It was our fault, anyway.

• It stresses the cat.

• It makes us frightening.

Now their stress level, *always part of the problem*, has been sent into the stratosphere. Not to mention taking an axe to the trust we are trying to build.

• That trust is what makes the cat want to please us.

Don't undermine our own greatest advantage. Because this is always the human's fault. I know this to be true because:

• Cats *want* to use their box.

Honestly, they do. Their instincts tell them to find some loose earth, dig in it, and use that as a bathroom. In our house, that best place is their litter box, full of loose, diggable stuff that is only for them.

For a cat to not use their litter box, especially when a cat is *going against their instincts* by going on shoes and bedspreads and under the stairs, means the cat is incredibly stressed by their litter box situation. Something is wrong somewhere.

A cat not using their box is like a big red distress flare shot into the sky. They are in trouble, and they need our help. If we are unable to pick up our cat's subtle hints about how their care is lacking, they are going to have to be more obvious to get our attention.

We interpret our cat's misbehavior as some kind of revenge or rebellion. They know we want them to use their litter box. They are refusing.

Yes on both counts. But it's not that they are rebelling against our reasonable requests. Misbehavior is usually the cat's way of demonstrating that something is terribly wrong with how their care is being handled. It is up to us to help them fix it.

We can get mad because the cat keeps not using their box, and increase our attempts to let the cat know we don't want them doing that. But the cat knows that. Then they will increase their attempts, to tell us that. Then their stress climbs, and makes the problem worse, and we are upset and angry and our stress climbs.

It is the wrong way to handle it.

Part of the pet deal is that we meet their needs. If we haven't given our cat something appropriate to use as a bathroom, they will have to find something that approximates what their instincts demand they find in a bathroom.

Cats do such things because, like a flare sent up into a night sky, it is hard to ignore. We are supposed to see their flare of distress, and help them out.

Desperation is what forces them into alternatives they don't really like. After all, we don't have to train the cat to use the litter box in the first place.

So what is stopping them? Probably us. We might be making one of the three biggest mistakes that lead to litter box problems.

1. Has the cat been altered?

• If the answer is no, it's no wonder there are problems.

Male or female, cats in the grip of their hormones can be driven to "mark their territory" by spraying especially stinky urine all over the house.

Male cats are almost guaranteed to exhibit this behavior, and with female cats it's more like 50-50. But maybe we've already thrown those dice, and lost. Even though it's less likely for females than males to exhibit this behavior, there are plenty of other reasons to alter the cat.

A female cat will wail for days on end when she's in heat, drawing every tomcat in a five mile radius to her vicinity. Male cats become desperate to roam and fight.

Cats driven by a frustrated mating urge can become aggressive and short-tempered, destroying our possessions and lashing out at innocent victims.

• Even if our intact cat isn't spraying now, there's no guarantee that they won't do it in the future.

Stress in the house, seeing other cats in their yard, or adding a new member to the household — any stress can trigger this behavior if there are still hormones circulating in the cat that tells them to do it.

When the male cat gets out he might come back injured from fighting. When the female cat gets out she will come back pregnant. Because she won't come back until she gets her body's "successful mating" signal that tells her she is pregnant.

Notice I'm saying when they get out, not if. Because they will get out. They are few organisms more determined to fulfill their genetic destiny than a cat in the grip of raging hormones.

• All the good will in the world won't change one of the cat's most basic drives.

I still maintain that matching the cat's natural instincts are the best way to live with a cat. So why is making such a radical change to the cat's reproductive potential something I consider a good thing?

• Because there isn't any other health choice, training regimen, or daily practice that can make such a difference to the cat's happiness and health as altering, which applies to either sex of cat.

• By removing the source of the hormones, we are also removing the impetus behind the behaviors, and the behaviors themselves.

What about cat breeders?

Ethical cat breeders will actively manage their female cats so they will not become pregnant until after a few heats, when they are more mature and ready for mothering. Then they follow up with medical care throughout the pregnancy.

In our home, the unaltered female cat is more likely to become pregnant at her first heat, at an age when she is at risk for health problems. This can cause serious complications and increases the chances of something going wrong with the pregnancy. This will all cost much more than timely spaying, and leave us with a litter of kittens who will need homes.

Good cat breeders take elaborate precautions so their male cats do not become a problem to themselves. The unaltered male pet will roam far in his quest to find willing lady cats, and will fight rivals.

They are at high risk to come home badly injured, or not come home at all.

Vet reluctance

One of the biggest, and most preventable, reasons for delay is the attitude of some veterinary professionals. It used to be standard procedure to wait until the cat was six months old, and I've encountered vets who want to wait until nine months.

In recent years, in an effort to combat cat overpopulation, shelters have been altering kittens at younger ages, and this led to the discovery that the kittens bounce back more quickly at younger ages, and there are no bad effects from doing it so young. It's called pediatric altering. Once the kitten is safely over two pounds, it can be done.

While large breeds like the Maine Coon and Norwegian Forest Cat can take up to three or four years to fully mature, the opposite is true of Alpha Cat Type breeds like the Siamese. Males can start developing physically, and start developing mating behaviors, as early as four months. With mixed breeds, the probable window of development is even more unknown. Which leads to another factor vets are mostly unaware of, but I have seen over and over again.

• The influence of early deprivation can cause the cat to reach sexual maturity more quickly.

If the kitten has been deprived or neglected early on, or their mother was during the pregnancy, the cat can mature earlier than they would under better circumstances. It's Mother Nature's way of ensuring cat survival when times are tough.

So if we know or suspect our kitten had been born and grew up under the burden of stress and inadequate nutrition, it's a signal we should move more quickly. The vet who wants to wait until the cat gets to be eight or nine months old might be putting us at risk for having a cat hormone problem.

Most of the time, vets had their training prior to these new discoveries, and like any profession, they can be reluctant to fix a system they think is not broken. However, their admission that they will quickly schedule it in case of "problems" means it certainly can be discussed now, with the goal of heading off problems.

Whenever we decide the best time to do it is, we must spay or neuter. There are already too many homeless cats in our world. If we want to make even one of them happy, we will spay or neuter. That is why they call it "fixed".

• There are programs that help people with the cost of this operation. Ask at the local shelter or contact *PAWS*.

• If the cat has been altered and still goes outside the litter box,

• See Page 195: Retrain a Cat with Their Litter Box.

No matter what we do, litter box problems are bound to happen with a cat who is still in the grip of their mating hormones. Isolate the cat before and after the operation, and then start fresh, with their new, adjusted, behaviors.

2. Is the cat sick?

If the cat has been altered, there can still be a physical reason for them not using the litter box. A great deal of the time, the cat is trying to say they are sick.

This is what I call the "beseeching gaze" where Tristan wants something.

Why don't people rush their cat to the vet the minute the cat stops using the litter box?

- They get upset with the cat.

- They don't know this is a cat sickness signal.

- The cat doesn't seem sick.

Don't bother saying to ourselves, "But the cat doesn't act sick."

- This is *how* the cat acts sick.

They aren't going to drag around, acting weak and under the weather. They are going to pretend they feel fine, even if they are anything but. The only signs are signals they send to their trusted human. These signals are changes in their usual routine. Including the all-important litter box.

Unfortunately, even people who notice the change in the cat's routine often don't know what the changes mean. Even obvious ones, like litter box problems. The cat can't help but react this way. Cats can be solitary in the wild, and their survival depends on them not acting sick. We take the cat out of the wild, but we cannot take the wild out of the cat.

That's why, when we bring a cat to the vet because they are acting like they feel lousy, the medical staff jumps right in, because they know this is one sick cat, maybe only hours away from death. That's how good cats are at hiding their illnesses.

So that must always be the first question we ask ourselves whenever our altered and otherwise happy cat deviates from their normal behavior, such as no longer using the litter box. Unless we've had the cat vet-checked recently, their medical condition must be the first thing to investigate.

- We can't do anything to fix a litter box problem unless it is *not a health problem*.

Why is this problem so common when it is also so easily fixable? Because the cat doesn't act sick. That's why, when cats come into the shelter with litter box problems, the first thing shelters do is have the cat checked by a veterinarian.

It's astonishing to find out how often the cat had an easily fixable infection. But by that time the cat owner is so sour on the situation they don't want the cat back, even when someone explains what is going on.

• Why does the cat stop using the litter box when they are sick?

Illness often makes the cat have pain when they eliminate. Since cats associate the pain with their litter box, this sends them on a useless and annoying quest to find a place they can go to the bathroom where it doesn't hurt.

If the problem is that the cat seems to go *everywhere*, this is a sign of the cat having bad associations with going *anywhere*. Each time they go to the bathroom and feel terrible, they will try to find a new place. Even if the cat isn't in pain from going to the litter box, they might still be in distress, and the way they communicate it is to not use the litter box.

Because we aren't going to ignore that, are we?

Cats don't know that their people might not understand this signal. From the cat's point of view, they have sent up a big **Red Flare of Distress**.

• That's why a distressed cat will leave signs of their distress right where we will find it.

People have asked me why the cat used their shoes or a pile of fresh laundry. They will exclaim, "The cat's not hiding it."

Well, that's right. The cat regards us as their protector, an all-knowing being who doesn't do anything unless it's on purpose. We know everything. Surely we will notice THIS, and know something is wrong with the cat.

• If only more people knew that's why the cat did that.

So if we find out the cat is sick, we can (hopefully) make the cat better. And know, next time, that this is a sign the cat is sick. Because, in a way, the cat is right. It's a signal we can't ignore.

So make an appointment right away, and tell the vet staff it's because they aren't using their litter box. If we have a sample to bring, and maybe we do, bring that too. These low level illnesses can hang on for months or longer, creating all sorts of mayhem that can be solved far more easily when they are caught right away.

Male cats can be particularly vulnerable to urinary tract infections, because of the kinks in their system that are part of the way their equipment works. But any cat can pick one up, and the way they can't help but signal their distress is to stop using the litter box, the seeming source of their pain. If the vet finds this common problem, it is one that can be fixed with some antibiotics.

• See page 209: Medicate a cat

Once the Cat is Well

• Often, clearing up the medical problem is all it takes. The cat feels good again, and starts right in with their box. Time to celebrate.

But if this doesn't completely solve the problem, we will have to reassure the cat, because now the cat might still associate the litter box with feeling sick.

• See page 195: Retrain a Cat with their Litter Box

And... there still might be litter box problems, and we have to remove them. Otherwise, the cat, under any kind of stress, will start sending up flares again.

So, are we making the third big litter box mistake?

3. Is the litter box clean?

We have to be brutally honest, because this is an emergency.

• How often do we clean the cat's litter box?

Because that is the dirty little secret of many litter box problems. Even if we would swear up and down in a court of law that we clean it every day, this is a crisis. Time for total honesty.

• Because two beings on earth know exactly how often we clean the litter box.

• One of them is us.

• The other is the cat.

• And we can't fool either of them.

If we aren't cleaning the litter every day, that can lead to problems. If we are often putting off the litter for too long, that's definitely a problem. We are reluctant to use a dirty bathroom. Why should the cat be any different?

To explain why it is so difficult for a cat to adjust to poor litter box housekeeping, we have to understand that the cat is still driven by their wild instincts, and they cannot go against them.

There's two ways to hide a predator from the sensitive noses of potential prey. Dogs chose the messy route of blending into background smells. This is why they love to roll in disgusting substances. *Hey, is that a wolf approaching? No, all I smell is that rotting carcass we passed a few trees back — yikes.*

Cats, perhaps because of their desert past offering relatively few disgusting, gooey, substances to roll in, have taken the opposite strategy. They continuously groom themselves to rid their presence of any telltale odors. One of the things we like about cats is their clean and tidy habits. So why would we create a situation where we expect a cat to use something that is repulsive to both us and them?

For a cat, being stinky, or hanging around something stinky, is something that will not only drive away the prey they need to eat, it will also announce their presence to bigger hunters who might want to eat them.

So we aren't merely asking the cat to use something that is their equivalent of the gas station washroom. We are also putting that less than appealing washroom in the middle of a Halloween haunted house.

It will make the cat nervous to be announcing their presence to other sensitive noses, as well as making them unhappy about their own sensitive nose.

• It not only helps the cat when we are fussy about their box. It helps us, too.

Why would we want something dirty and smelly in our house or apartment? Because it doesn't matter how much we use sprays or candles or other things to mask the scent. None of them work. The only way to get rid of the offending substances is to get rid of the offending substances.

• Resolve to do better.

Create an inviting litter box

Even if we keep the litter box clean, there can be other sources of distress for the cat.

This is where a lot of litter box problems start, and continue. From the human's point of view, the litter box is something that should be as far away as possible. Like down in the basement, or out in the garage, or in some other remote place.

I understand the thinking, believe me, but we might have traded cosmetic problems for worse ones.

• We've put the litter box in a place that is easy to ignore.

• We're ignoring it.

It's asking for trouble if the cat's litter box is hard for the cat to reach and use. Imagine if we had to use the bathroom and it is where we have put the cat's bathroom. Go ahead, imagine it is the middle of the night, and we have to go through the whole house and down the stairs and do we have light for this journey? Cats see in the dark, yes, but not in total dark. Do we have to step over the dog or negotiate through all those boxes we store there?

How did we feel about it?

There's a reason indoor plumbing was invented, and a reason most houses have bathrooms on every floor. Because no one likes to run an obstacle course at a time like this.

Maybe we don't realize the cat spends a lot of their time waiting for the right doors to be open, or the dog to be out, or the toddlers down for their nap. Many factors might affect their ability, to make it through the whole obstacle course in time. Even if they make it this time, there's next time. This is a highly stressful situation, and sometimes the cat just can't handle that when they need to go.

• Don't make our cat run an obstacle course.

We might not know of other problems, having stuck the litter box in a place we visit as little as possible.

What if the furnace suddenly comes on at a crucial time? Do the neighbors turn their yard lights on at night, so we don't realize the cat's box is spotlighted in high voltage, making the cat feel like an escaped prisoner when they go there at night? Maybe there are smelly rags or paint or other stinky stuff stored there, or something else that smells like skunk fumes to the cat's sensitive nose, even if we don't notice.

These are all things that cats hate. They want to be able to relax in their box. For them, as for us, this is a vulnerable time and place they hate to feel nervous about.

Out of sight, out of mind

A remote box is popular because we don't have to think about it very often. But that same remoteness could be working against us.

We don't notice if the box is dirty. If we find it a hassle to visit a remote box for cleaning every day, how do we think the cat feels, visiting it more than once a day, and finding it in sorry shape when they do get there?

I repeat, *the cat wants to use their box*. Most cats will use their box even when conditions are pretty bad. But letting a marginal litter box situation go on means if there is one little added stress in the house, then the cat can't take it anymore.

We know how it is. When we are having a bad day, finding out there's no creamer for our coffee can be enough to make us feel like snapping at someone, even though it's a small thing. But it's not a small thing when it comes at the end of a line of piled up annoyances.

If the cat finds using their box to be stressful, they will still try to use it. That's their normal instinct. But add on some other stresses, like a new baby, new puppy, health crisis for the humans, or simply not having enough time for the cat and making them lonely; any stress can make that unappealing litter box too much to handle.

Cats are sensitive creatures. They simply hide it well. But stress will always appear, usually at the worst time, and in the worst way.

People do all kinds of crazy things that are actually more trouble than cleaning the box. They don't clean it until they practically have to don one of those plastic suits to go near it. They plug in several air fresheners. They throw out the entire box and start over.

All of these things are incredibly stressful for the cat. It's no surprise that, at some point, the cat throws in the towel.

Don't protest that the cat has always used their box in its rotten location and in its sorry state. That only means the cat has been going out on a limb for us all this time, putting up with all kinds of things.

Maybe the cat is a bit older now, and less able to manage that obstacle course. Maybe the house is rowdier than it used to be, and the cat is dealing with more. Whatever the reason, if there's anything we can do to improve the situation, improve it.

We owe the cat.

• We've found out there are worse things than cleaning a litter box every day, haven't we?

Because, properly set up, a cat box should take maybe five minutes a day, no more. That includes sweeping up the scatter, tying two knots in the bag where we have put the ugly stuff, adding litter, and sprinkling baking soda. With practice, we can cut that time even more.

We simply have to decide to do it. And we have to set the box up better.

Have an invisible litter box

Keep any needed tools beside the litter; fresh litter, a little dustpan and brush to sweep up scatter, the bags, the scoop, the baking soda. Anything we have to go and get will slow us down and make us put the task off to another time.

Get a shelf system or cabinet to hold the tools, or screen it. We can make the whole setup as unobtrusive as possible, but it must be a whole setup.

This is how we can make cleaning the litter a task that can be undertaken like a commando raid: *get in and get out.*

This kind of system removes odors before they spread, makes the box easier to contemplate at any time, and encourages us to clean the litter often.

This make tidying up before guests come only one simple step instead of a big additional task. With both a system and a schedule, neither we nor the cat ever has to face a daunting mess.

• Because the real objection anyone has to the litter is the smell.

Cleaning the litter removes the smell; better than deodorizers, sprays, plug-ins, or candles. Better than anything.

Go over this list, and see if we are making any of these other litter box mistakes:

—*Scented litter.* Air fresheners, or other things to cover up the smell. These actually work against us. The cat's nose is far more sensitive than ours is. What we think is the pleasant smell of flowers is, to the cat, like having a vat of eye-watering perfume sharing their bathroom.

Worse, this can confuse the cat, since ideally the cat box should smell like... fresh, unscented, litter. They are going to worry that they aren't supposed to use this weird smelling object, and then they don't.

Likewise, don't use strong smelling cleaners to clean the litter box. No matter how we rinse, the smell might remain. Plain soap and water will work as well, and not confuse the cat.

—*Litter that isn't soft and sandlike.* If the granules are too large and sharp-edged, it can be like walking on a gravel road for the cat's sensitive paws. There are also pine pellets, wood shavings, and other variations on the sandbox theme. And some cats get along with them fine.

But they are not what the cat instinctively looks for. They might use it, because it's in their box, but there will be a nagging thought in the back of their head that they really shouldn't be whizzing on this stuff.

We do want them sensitive to what they are whizzing on, don't we? It can be a mistake to make them wonder if their litter is something they are supposed to use.

—*Wrong size or shape of box.* If the cat is missing the box, or scattering a lot of litter around, or leaving stuff on the edges, the box is too small. The cat thinks they are in the right area, but the business end is not.

Get a bigger box, and don't fool ourselves thinking bigger means more intrusive. What's more objectionable— a small, messy box, surrounded by litter dunes, or a big box with all the mess inside, coated with litter for easy pick up?

Don't make the mistake of minimizing what is needed for a clean box by thinking we can make its footprint smaller. It's purpose is important to both ourselves and our cat, and deserves as much room as the situation requires, not less.

—*Deeper is better.* We want the cat to bury their leavings, don't we? So make it easy for them. All cat professionals swear by the deep boxes.

It's rare for the clumps to get stuck on the bottom or the sides that way. Then the cat can dig, and cover, and feel like they've accomplished something. This also contains the smell. It's a win-win.

If we have a very young or old cat, we might have to add a ramp so they can get in and out, but it's worth it to have a deep box.

—*Make it slick.* For some weird reason, a lot of litter boxes have a rough surface. Don't fall for it. Get one as slick as possible for easy cleanup.

—*Not enough privacy.* Don't put the box in a busy area. This is as objectionable as squeezing the cat's box into a space where they can't see what's around them. Having a lot of people in and out of the room their box is in can keep them from using it when they need to.

Retrain with their litter box

Naturally, we will want to eliminate reminders around the house. We don't want them around, and we don't want them to remind the cat, either.

• See page 208: Clean Up After the Cat for more about getting rid of these reminders.

If the cat wasn't sick, or the cat is better but still avoiding their box, then something else is wrong with the litter box situation, from the cat's point of view.

We can signal the change by doing a complete clean of the litter box, maybe move some of the things around it, anything we can do to signal that this is a new litter situation, and one they can trust.

• Cats are sensitive to environmental cues. A small change to us can signal a big change to the cat.

Is anything arranged to annoy the cat while they are in their box? Since we tend to put the litter box in places we don't spend a lot of time, or in storage rooms, a lamp put away in the room can seem to hang over the box, or we could have pushed furniture and boxes around so that the cat feels like they are at the end of a tunnel with their litter box.

Even if we can't figure out what the cat is telling us, we should move some stuff around to show we are making a good faith effort to address their concerns. We might fix it, or our concern can be enough to reassure the cat that this is a good spot for them.

Maybe a bunch of boxes got stacked near it, and now the cat feels loomed over. Maybe we hung some wind chimes in the window, and the sudden noises or shadows moving over the cat makes them feel nervous. Maybe we put an air freshener in the room and to the cat the smell is overwhelming.

If something has changed, try to make the room back into what it was when the cat was happy there. Things we might not notice are big environmental cues to our cat. They love to patrol their territory and know the location of everything in it.

Rearranging the furniture while not touching the box has still, to them, changed the box. The sight lines could be different, the shadows could be different, the route they take to get to the box could be different.

• What the cat is asking for is what they are getting from wherever they are eliminating instead of the litter box.

If it's the corner of a closet, they want a quieter spot than the one they have now. If it's the middle of a room, they want a wide field of view. If it's on the way to the litter box, such as the steps to the basement where the litter box resides, it's too much of a hike to ask of them.

We could also have changed the litter we are buying, or need to change the litter we are buying. If we changed it, change it back. If it works, saving a bit on sale is not worth the torment.

• If all else fails, we can put the litter box *where the cat wants to go.*

This isn't as crazy as it sounds. Yes, it's nasty, temporarily, but still better than finding it elsewhere. This move can be an important part of retraining the cat to use the box. If, for some reason, the cat has been freaked out over their box, they can form an aversion to the place where the box is. We can retrain them to get over it, but we will need to put the box somewhere else, anyway.

If the cat is insistent on using one place, which is not where the box is, putting the box where the cat has been going will at least improve our cleanup tasks.

• If we can get the box used again, the cat is halfway back to proper training.

• Then we can move the box and see if the cat follows it. By the time the box gets to where it's supposed to go, or maybe a new, better, place, the cat will move with it and feel better about things.

• Once the box is no longer there, leave food in the places where the cat has been eliminating. This sends the "not litter box" signal about the area.

Once the box has moved out of the area, close off the rooms where the cat has been desperate before, so they no longer have access to them. If we had the cat alone in a room, and got litter box compliance that way, we have a vital clue about what has been going on. Part of the problem is that the cat is nervous and insecure about the previous spot.

Something is making the cat reluctant to use their litter where it was, since when the cat is alone in the room with the litter, they use it. What we have done is turn down the volume of possible stress, so the cat is better able to cope.

This works best with nervous, insecure cats. They can feel overwhelmed being left alone in the place all day. In a desperate attempt to mark territory, they can start going in places where they feel safe.

The space we confine them in can be very small. Some people have had success with kenneling, where they put the cat in a big dog crate and only let them out when they can be supervised. There is only a bed and a litter box in the crate. If the cat is always using the box when we are home, and not using it when we are away from home, this can be a good retraining step.

It's not cruel. Cats like these have to calm down. Marking out a small space for them, where they feel safe, can be the kindest thing we can do. As they gain confidence, they can be let out more and more, until the whole place feels comfortable for them, and they will have the confidence to use all their different places.

If space is limited, consider using our bathroom for times when we are away from home. Maybe the cat litter is already there. If we lock the cat in the room, and then they use it, we know it's a nervous issue.

They can't handle big spaces yet.

Here, we expanded to two Robots. No waiting. Tristan inspects the new arrival.

Calm the cat

Since so many litter box issues come from the nervous, insecure cat, we should also take steps to calm the cat and build up their confidence.

—*Feliway diffusers.* This is a scentless (to us) pheromone that broadcasts "Everything is okay," in cat scent language. It has worked miracles for some people's cats. Some of the bigger pet stores carry it, but we can always find it on the Internet.

—*Rescue Remedy.* This is a flower essence that is common in rescue work. We can put it in their water. No one is sure exactly how it works, but it does seem to work. Don't be afraid to hit it ourselves when it seems like it's all too much. Almost any health food store will have it, and also the Internet.

—*Littermint.* This is our own product, an organic, litter additive that communicates "freshness" to the cat. Try a bag to add to the litter after cleaning.

—*Police the situation.* If other cats are being too assertive with our timid cat, we must warn off the more confident cats, and fuss over the shy one. It can be as simple as escorting them to the litter box a few times, and reminding the other cats that the shy one has equal claim as all the other cats.

—*Burning off energy.* Take the time each day to play with the cat, and don't be afraid to get them worked up. Running, jumping, and leaping will take their mind off their troubles, and build their confidence.

Being hunters is part of who they are. Help the cat reach that part of themselves, and they will feel better, and sleep better. A play session will help burn up the energy that is pushing their nerves into overdrive.

After we make changes, introduce the cat to their litter as though it were new. Act happy and attentive. See what they say with their body language.

Find out which cat

With more cats, the litter box setup might mean additional stresses to varying degrees because of the cat's territorial nature. These instincts, depending on the individual cat, can run the range from happily using the same box, to keeping another cat from sharing their favorite box, to not sharing boxes at all.

Two cats will share a litter box if we put in the effort to clean it often. If each cat feels they have an equal shot at getting a clean box, there will be less competition. If we have more cats and have the room, an extra box placed somewhere is a great option to please all the cats all the time.

The extra box doesn't necessarily need the same set of tools, if it's easy to carry them from one to the other to make sure both boxes are cleaned every time.

One rule of thumb for multiple cats is: a box for every cat, and one extra. Yet, I have three cats who share one litter box. How can this be?

My litter box is automatic, a *Litter Robot*. Seven minutes after a cat uses it, it is cleaned and a brand new litter box is ready for the next cat.

So, with multiple cats, we can solve our problem by coming up with ways for every cat to get the kind of box they need. One might care more about privacy, one could care more about easy access, and another can be fussy about how clean the box is. If we can come up with a way of meeting everyone's needs, we can find the best option for us.

Multiple cat homes have another challenge. How can we tell which cat is sending up the distress signals?

We should start with any cat who is showing other signs of distress and isolate them with a litter box. Changes in any other cat's behavior can be a clue, too.

Often, the cat who is having the most trouble using the litter box will be the shyest cat, or the highly wound cat who is showing signs of frustration. A cat who is getting enough activity and the proper diet will be more forgiving of litter box mistakes than a cat who is under extra stress.

• It might take a few rounds, but we can always find the problem cat with systematic isolation away from other stressors.

We can then take the proper steps. If it is the other cats guarding the litter box, or using it as an excuse for playtime, the distressed cat needs support from us to be happy using their litter box. Adding an extra box, designed to address their issues, can be exactly the right move.

It's better to have three clean boxes than one dirty one. There's little extra time involved when we consider the challenge of tackling the dirty one. Or perhaps the main box should go on a twice a day schedule if we would prefer that to another box.

Stressing the cat may not cause litter box problems. But it makes any litter box problem much worse.

Litter **box signals**

Much of the time, the Three Biggest Mistakes are all that's needed to correct a Litter Box Problem.

But what if we have corrected these, and the problem still continues? What if we never made those mistakes, and still have a problem? What could be going wrong?

We will develop skills that will always come in handy.

—*We will listen to the cat.* Cats send up signals if they are having litter box distress. We must look for these signals and understand what they mean. What does the cat say when the litter situation is making them nervous?

—*The cat rushes away from the litter box.* If the cat dashes out of the room or takes off from the box, this can be a sign that visiting the box is stressful. The cat feels such a sense of relief, once they know they can leave this upsetting situation, that they run away from it.

—*Cat wailing near the box.* Something about the box is upsetting them, and they are trying to tell us. Don't think we can't figure out what the cat is saying. We should ask them what is going on and follow them to the box where we can look around to see if anything has changed.

—*Cat using the dining room instead of their box.* Why is the dining room such a popular spot for this kind of cat misbehavior? While there's no denying there's something extra upsetting about this behavior, we have to remember that the cat does not see it the same way we do. Sure we eat there, but in a lot of households, it's not all that often.

To the cat, the dining room is little used, relatively open so they can see all around them, and a place they know they will not be disturbed. *This,* the cat is saying, is what they want from their litter box.

—*Cat going on the bed.* This is usually an insecure cat, who wants to go somewhere they feel safe. Unfortunately, we don't feel complimented. It can also be an attempt to mark us and our things as their own.

• If we routinely launder with bleach, or a scented soap or softener, stop.

Bleach can send a pheromone to the cat that their brains interpret as "go here". Leave the bleach or scents out of the bed linens for a few cycles and see if this affects the problem.

—*Hooded box signals.* We find the hood askew, or litter scattered all over the floor. We like it because we can't see the litter. But the cat might dislike it for that same reason. Some of the hooded boxes I've seen would make an average-sized cat claustrophobic. Some of them like to see what's around them when they are in the litter.

• Getting snuck up on in the litter box is every cat's secret fear, just as every human's secret fear is the shower scene in *Psycho*.

Don't feed that fear.

Automatic litter box

I know how compelling a clean cat litter box can be. That's because there are thousands of cats successfully using automatic litter boxes which have flashing lights, moving parts, and motor noises. Cats will overcome their dislike of such scary appliances because:

- These devices keep the litter cleaner.

- Clean litter is so attractive cats will put up with a lot to use it.

So if keeping up with the litter is a chore we dread, consider getting some automated help which won't whine and complain and put it off for another day. Especially if that person is us.

I haven't tried every automatic litter device on the market. That's because I would look at most of them and instantly know all the ways they could go wrong, causing more trouble than they are worth. I'm not going to pay money to have more litter troubles.

- Choosing the right kind is a vital step to success.

At one time, cat boxes were actually filled with sand. It wasn't until 1984, when clumping bentonite was developed by biochemist Thomas Nelson, that the age of cat litter robotics began.

Based on clumping litter

Clumping litter is a marvelous invention. It makes cleaning go faster and the offending lumps are less odor-prone. Don't get the scented kind. I've found a scattering of baking soda works well and cats don't object to it.

I have done time in the litter mines. With my previous cat rescue, I had +/- ten cats at any given time. I used to maintain four big boxes. Every day. Before there was scooping litter. Hard, hard time.

I used to gird for the task by reminding myself that I did it out of love. There was also the not inconsiderable enjoyment of visitors exclaiming that they couldn't tell that we had any cats at all, judging from the atmosphere.

I marveled at the relative ease clumping litter brought to the task. It ushered in the Search for the Automatic Cat Box Grail.

- A cat box that would clean itself.

Online reviews are full of stories of cats startled by the grinding of litter-clogged parts and confused by the wails of stuck rakes. But in my heart, there was still hope.

When a friend expressed her own despair over the litter situation, I promised to see what had happened in the intervening years. Automation offers the next great step in the cat lover's dream, I explained to my friend, but so far I could not recommend anything I had heard of. I even got on the Internet later to research her options.

I found the Grail.

- I choose the *Litter Robot*.

Because the Litter Robot works. Constantly, quietly, and consistently.

So I recommend the Litter Robot without reservation. Yes, it's big. As large as two litter boxes side by side, and about two and half feet tall. It needs an electrical outlet. It's enclosed, but it's bigger than any other enclosed box I've seen.

How much would we pay to have the litter box cleaned every time the cat used it? So that our chore is replacing the bag every week for one cat? To have no litter smell and no ugly chores every day?

It uses minimal electricity, cheap 13 gallon trash bags we can get at any grocery store, and can cut our litter usage by almost half.

Tristan adapted to the Litter Robot right away. Here, he inspects a newly unboxed Open Air model.

So, yes, I'm saying we should get a pricey automatic litter box. Our first Litter Robot was a reconditioned unit, and between litter savings and the discount, I calculated that it cost between six and seven dollars a month over its lifetime.

Don't make the same mistake so many other people make, getting a cheaper automatic litter box... that has to be replaced every year, or sooner, because it's badly designed and doesn't do the job, anyway. Buying the cheaper box, and then picking cat poo out of the rake every week.

And say goodbye to litter chores. Make everyone happy... for less than a trip to a fast food place once a month.

We pay that, and more, for other appliances, don't we? Well, that's what the Litter Robot does. It cleans the litter for us, every time, and deposits the clumps in a sealed drawer at the bottom. Litter chores are then as easy as emptying the other bathroom trash.

Wouldn't we pay some small sum a month for that kind of ease and convenience?

Of course we would. In a heartbeat.

Curious? The Litter Robot site is www.litter-robot.com, where they have videos that shows how it works, a payment plan, and a 60 day money back guarantee.

Tell them the *Way of Cats* sent you.

Clean up after the cat

When we have a cat going where they shouldn't, we must take some extra pains with cleanup, so they do not act as reminders.

We will need two things:

• A black light, for finding dried areas that would otherwise be overlooked

• Enzyme cleaner, marketed to remove odors and stains

Really soak the areas for the enzyme cleaner to do its best work. If the floors or other places are going to have trouble with all this fluid, give it 30-60 minutes, and then soak up the excess.

Late at night, with no other light, go over any suspect areas with the black light. Don't freak out over what we find. It will fluoresce at any biological source, so while it seems the cat has been going crazy, *not all of them are cat spots*. These spots will need the enzyme cleaner anyway.

Another good cleaning solution is to use one part white vinegar with five parts water, and a dash of dishwashing soap. This is good for carpets and upholstery. Sturdier surfaces, such as floors that can be mopped, should get the vinegar treatment at a higher strength, then rinsed well.

Medicate a cat

If we have the choice between liquid or pills, get the liquid. Easier on everyone.

While we are at the vet, ask them to demonstrate the best method, and take any tips they might offer for handling the cat.

For procedure, it depends on two factors; how comfortable our cat is about being wrestled with, and how invasive the medicine is going to be.

• Be safe, and recruit some stout-hearted person to help.

• If that is not possible, don't cut any corners with the process.

Have the medicine on us, such as in a shirt pocket. We need to spring onto the cat and get the medicine in them before they can get panicky. The faster we do it, the faster we will be forgiven.

Go to where the cat is. Do not call them, unless we want them to never come when called again. It's not fair to wait until they are cuddling with us, or otherwise enjoying a happy moment, and then spring it on them, thinking they won't mind. They will mind, and distrust happy moments for a while after that. Don't abuse their trust.

• Hunt them down, don't interrupt a happy moment.

Grasp the cat by their back of the neck, gathering up some of the loose skin. We work on the floor or the sofa, wherever the cat may be. Avoid countertops if we are alone; cats can grab the edge of the counter with their rear feet and get away from us. We have the medicine on our person, so we don't have to transport a suspicious cat somewhere.

If the cat is the struggling type, have a towel to wrap around them and immobilize their legs. We can pin down the edges of the towel with our knees if we are working on the floor.

Using the other hand (don't let go of the back of their neck) we tilt the cat's head to one side and can squirt the liquid into their mouth, between their teeth.

If a pill, we need to palm the pill, and gently tilt their head upward. Open their mouth with gentle, steady, pressure on their cheeks against their teeth. We can then drop the pill down the back of their throat.

In either case, help swallowing by closing their mouth, keeping their head tilted upward, and stroking their neck until we feel them swallow.

Afterwards, apologize, and remind them we want them to get better. Maybe they don't know exactly what we are saying, but they understand the tones of our voice and our body language better than we can imagine.

Later, when they start to feel better, they will connect it with our actions. They still won't like it, but they won't hold a grudge.

Feeding the wrong food?

It might seem silly to talk about food or water problems with our pet. We put the bowl down, they eat and drink, what's the problem?

Indeed, if we have a dog, these problems are rare. Dogs are famous for eating whatever they can get and drinking out of the toilet. But cats are not dogs. There's your problem.

If we are used to dogs and their not-fussy ways, cats can seem like a big puzzle.

- Why won't they eat the food we give them?

- Why won't they stop asking for food, even if they have some?

- Why won't they drink their water?

- Why won't they leave our tasty beverages alone?

- What is going on?

Cats have very survival strategies than dogs do. That's why they are so fussy about their food and water needs. This is, once again, a life or death issue for them. They can't change what they need.

—*Changing their food.* Call them into their eating area for some canned food, and freshen their water bowl. Be happy about it. No canned food? (There's your problem.) Give them some tuna or other canned fish, or mince up uncured deli meats like roast beef, chicken, or turkey. Add a bit of butter on top.

The hungry cat and the fat cat need more protein and fat. Cats and dogs are both hunters, but what they eat, how they have to eat it, and how they catch it, are totally different.

Dogs hunt, and eat, in packs. That's why dogs have a tendency to "wolf" down their food. They are always eating with others around, and it's boarding house rules, (if you grab it, it's yours). Dogs are also opportunistic eaters; they hunt and eat meat, but they can also eat plants, or even scavenge from whatever is around.

That's why our pet dogs will eat whatever we are eating, and often prefer to. That's why our pet dogs will drink from almost any source; they are used to abundant sources of water. They are not fussy, since they don't have to be fussy.

• Cats do have to be fussy. They are built that way.

Cats mostly hunt alone. Once they catch fresh prey, they eat it right away. Cats are not scavengers. They do not store food for later, and cannot eat anything that seems "off" to their sensitive noses. Cats came from the desert, where water can be stale, contaminated, and deadly. So they need their water to be as fresh and pure as possible.

How do these needs conflict with what their humans offer them?

Many people don't know about cat feeding habits. We might be making some of the biggest mistakes that lead to food and water problems.

Pet food myths

When I started reading the labels for the food I'd been feeding my cats, I was truly astonished at how many ingredients were grain based, and how low down the list I had to go before the meat products appeared. It's not like the label makes it easy.

• Pet food regulations do not allow the word carbohydrate on the label.

To get the carb content, pet parents have to take a calculator to that information on the label:

100- (protein + fat + moisture + ash + fiber) = carb content

Those bags I was buying at the supermarket were not much more than enriched, meat-frosted, breakfast cereal.

Which is why the pet food companies make a meat-flavored spray to coat the food and get the cat to eat it. It's like Frosted Flakes, only for cats.

With the cat's sense of smell (fourteen times more sensitive than our own) telling them it's meat, they will eat it. But their body is not so easily fooled.

Most dry cat foods are loaded with grains, which are mostly carbohydrates. Because the cereal ingredients gets processed at high heat and pressure to make those charming shapes, it becomes somewhat pre-digested and enters the cat's bloodstream essentially as sugar.

Our cat is not equipped to handle a steady influx of sugar in their bloodstream. This can strain the cat's obligate carnivore digestive system.

Wrong food signals

The cat uses their wild instincts as a system of realizing they are full. Only the consumption of *fat and protein* will trip the signal to the cat that they can stop eating now.

If the cat is fed a diet heavy with carbohydrate, they can't use that intake to signal their bodies they have eaten enough. If they are eating carbohydrate, which has no usable nutrients, they will overeat until they get enough protein and fat, the only nutrients which trigger their satiety signal.

They manage with the minimal amounts of meat in most cat foods, but those extra, empty, calories make them:

• Eat more, since their body is telling them it is still hungry. This can make a cat drive us crazy asking for food.

• Get fat, since their body can only store the grains as fat. In the meantime, the cat lacks protein. They only look well-fed.

• Get sick, since they are lacking nutrients and putting stress on their body.

Cats get digestive troubles from a high carbohydrate intake. They throw up more, have diarrhea and constipation, and eventually get diabetes from the pancreas overload. This all turns out to be more expensive and more heartbreaking than giving the cat their proper food, which is meat.

• If we aren't feeding canned food, start. If we are feeding canned food, feed it more.

Best choices

There are high protein dry foods on the market that we can add to the cat's diet, but these are best for:

• The cat might be stuck on the dry food, and needs something to ease the transition.

• Leaving a dish out for the cat to nibble on. Many cats find this comforting, even if they don't eat much.

But choose the dry food carefully. Look for grain-free. There are a number of companies now offering dry food with much more meat in them. The same rule applies: the first ingredient, or more, should be meat. Check at pet supply stores, who are usually glad to order something and keep it in stock. Especially after we tell all our friends where to get the better food.

It can be a long process to transition cats to a new food. That's because, as young cats, they learn what is good to eat. Then they stop. So cats are often suspicious of new food.

Mix the new food into the old food gradually, increasing their proportions as the cat accepts it. Mix canned into their old dry, and move them away from it that way. Use a trick the food companies use, and add some tuna juice or broth to make the food more appealing at first.

• Cats can and do change their minds. It happens more slowly than humans like, that's all.

When the cat is on a good diet of canned, and maybe some dry food that we chose for its high meat content, we will be amazed at their sleek and shiny fur, their solid bodies that aren't too fat, and their relaxed and lively personality.

It's not only their bodies that suffer when their food is not good for them. A chronically hungry cat who doesn't feel well can be a more cranky and unfriendly pet.

One last tip, especially for cats who live indoors, is to grow them some "kitty grass" in pots on the windowsill.

• See page 225: Grow Kitty Grass for instructions

Investing in our cat's food is like paying an insurance policy. We might get sticker shock comparing the prices of the better food to what we get at the grocery store. There's a few things to keep in mind that puts this situation in perspective.

When we get the high quality food from specialty pet stores or feed stores, we are getting what we pay for. Our distress at comparing prices is because we are thinking of the bags or cans as having equal amounts of food. But our calculator trick tells us that isn't so.

It's not as expensive as it might seem. My cats *ate less* of the nutrient dense, better food. I wasn't going out and having to get it as often.

So when we go searching for better foods, go by what the calculations tells us. The less carbohydrates in the food, the more protein and fat there will be in what we are buying. That's what we should be paying for, since cats need the protein and fat.

The rest will only make them sick.

Are we making the cat thirsty?

If the cat is driving us crazy by playing in their water bowl, tipping it over, going after our drinks, and leaping in the shower after we are done, they aren't doing it to be annoying.

• They are thirsty.

Cats are often thirsty because people think leaving out a bowl of water is enough. But it's not. Would we drink water that is stale and has crumbs in it? Don't expect the cat to, either.

—*Don't put their water dish right next to their food.* A space between them will keep the water fresher. Do wash their water bowl as often as we clean their food bowl, and rinse well. Don't use plastic bowls, because this can make the water taste like plastic. If we use a filtering pitcher because it makes our water taste better, do it for the cats, too.

The cat can't help looking for running water over other sources, because their instincts tell them that is the freshest and safest. This is why many cat people use pet fountains, because then they know their cat will drink more of the fresher water.

I've found that a cat's fascination with our drinks can be turned to our advantage. We picked up some cheap, giant, coffee mugs, the wide kind used in coffee houses. This is the cat's water dish in the kitchen, and we've placed another one in the living room, where we hang out and the cats like to hang out with us. The cats like the feeling they are getting the same stuff we are drinking, from the same kinds of containers.

If we don't see the cat's water bowl drunk low or empty, then we haven't been offering water often enough, or making it clean enough. Water is vital for a cat's good health. Their high protein diet means their kidneys need a lot of water to keep their system operating at peak. So turn on that faucet, and make the cat happy.

Dining tips

The cat is going to be dependent on us to feed them, and in their natural state this is something they are used to doing for themselves.

• The more autonomy and control we give the cat over this process, the happier the cat will be.

The kitchen is the natural place to put their dining area, but make sure it's in a spot that won't get a lot of traffic. Cats have predatory instincts about their food.

• The reflexes defending their kill can be tripped by interruptions or a noisy dishwasher.

If our kitchen tends to be a busy place, pick another spot for them. It will make mealtime more enjoyable, and then they are not going to gulp down their food in a hurry and have digestive upsets.

Unlike dogs, they don't prefer gobbling down their meal with a bunch of others around. They naturally tend to take their prey to a quiet spot and take their time.

—*Choose ceramic, stainless steel, or glass bowls.* The cheap plastic bowls are too light. They are more likely to get spilled and knocked around. Their softness makes it harder to get them clean. They will then retain odors, which will spoil the cat's appetite.

—*Choose wide, shallow types.* Eating from a deep, narrow bowl impedes the cat's eating process, since they need to move their face from side to side when they eat. Also, many cats hate to pull up their whiskers while they eat. Sticking their face into a bowl also cuts off their vision, and they will feel vulnerable while they are eating. No one likes that.

—*Choose separate dishes for food and water.* Don't get the double feeding stations that have the water bowl right next to the food bowl. This is asking for the water bowl to get stuff in it, and spoil the freshness cats like.

We can't wash them separately, so they are less convenient. If the water is full of bloated food, and the food dish is still half full, we'll have to dump the food elsewhere while we wash the whole thing. This can make us put off the washing it needs.

—*Have at least two sets.* This way we won't postpone the washing up, especially since canned cat food might need soaking if they leave any behind overnight.

Olwyn was the first to love our cat fountain. From Thirsty Cat.

We don't have to get the cutesy bowls with happy cartoon cats on them, but we should choose a distinctive set of bowls that is only for the cat's use.

This will become part of their enjoyment of mealtime, and keeps them from having false expectations when we pull out dishes for our own use.

—*Get a mat to mark out the cat's dining area.* They are sensitive to such cues, and appreciate it. I like those dish drainer mats. They have a lip to corral the crumbs, they are easy to wash, and the non-slip surface means the bowls won't skate around from enthusiastic use.

Of course, if there are dogs or crawling babies around, put the food up high, out of a poacher's reach. Kittens that can't yet jump that high might need their food on the floor behind a baby gate or a closed door until they grow larger.

Nutrition strategies

Whether it's a kitten who needs extra help, like Reverend Jim, or a senior who is slowing down, like my beloved James Bond in his twilight years, extra nutrition can be a way of making sure enough nutrients get to where they need to go.

James Bond, at 18 years old, which is a fine accomplishment for a male cat his size.

For as long as I've had cats, people have come in and exclaimed over their apparently-incredible size. Since my cats have usually come to me totally at random, it's not that I'm picking large cats. I often get them at ages where it would be difficult to tell if they are going to be large or small ones.

I tend to max out a given cat's genetic heritage. I take that as a compliment.

Of all I do for my cats, I've found nutritional intervention to be both incredibly powerful, and completely made of upside.

—*Grain-free.* This isn't a supplement — it's what our cat's food *should not have.* But this is a case of nothing being so powerful as an element we want to leave out.

In nature, cats don't eat grains. Period. So feeding it to them in whatever form is not doing them any favors. They don't have the enzymes to digest it, it stresses systems like the pancreas, which leads to diabetes, and the intestines, where it can make them prone to constipation. Grain phytate content blocks the absorption of B vitamins, something cats already don't get enough of.

—*Brewer's yeast.* The beauty of this supplement is the high B complex content. It is also a good source of rare minerals, like chromium and selenium, which help the cat's metabolism.

Administration couldn't be easier, because my cats seem to like it. A 1/4 teaspoon mixed into their canned food, or tossed with their grain-free dry, is all it takes.

—*Spirulina.* All the things that's great about brewer's yeast is multiplied in this blue-green powder. It's 65% protein, which doesn't matter very much because it is ingested in small amounts.

What does matter is the abundance of bio-available vitamins and minerals: GLA, B-1(thiamine), B-2 (riboflavin), B-3 (nicotinamide), B-6 (pyridoxine), B-9 (folic acid), vitamin C, vitamin D, vitamin A, vitamin E, potassium, calcium, chromium, copper, iron, magnesium, manganese, phosphorus, selenium, sodium, zinc, and beneficial fatty acids.

• There's some accounts of cats doing well even with Chronic Kidney Failure when their diet was supplemented with Spirulina.

—*Good fats.* All cat foods tend to be too low in fat, since this is a fragile macronutrient and goes bad easily. But cats need the fat in their diets; and it will not make them fat.

I've long used coconut oil without a problem, in pea-sized amounts in their food dish. Butter, especially grass-fed butter, is something many cats like, and has a good Omega 3 profile from the grass being eaten by the cows.

Oily fish is a great source of good fats. If our cat likes salmon or sardines, make this a steady treat. There's also Omega 3 supplements available. Whenever we use a concentrated source, be sure to read the directions and follow them.

—*Dry gelatin & bone broth.* Until we start finding packages of whole rats in our pet shop's freezer case (and let's be honest, how many of us want to?) bones is a category of food our cats get in nature that is rather different in food we can buy.

In most cat foods, it is cooked down into an ashy substance (yes, that's the ash content on the label). At one time ash was considered a probable cause of feline urinary issues, but the latest thinking is that too much vegetable and grain content creates a more alkaline environment, unlike the high-protein, acidic state found in nature.

I discovered the power of dry gelatin when I was treating my elderly cat for arthritis. He began jumping from the bureau to the bed to show me how much better he felt.

—*Meats and organ meats.* Feeding cats people food is only a problem if the people food is not good for them. Meat is usually a great thing for us to share.

The only problems I've run into is with heavily salted or processed meats like bacon or ham. Fresh meat, prepared without spices or sauce, is an excellent addition to a cat's food dish. Organ meats like chicken livers or those beef bones full of marrow can be simmered into broth, and both are good for our cats.

Such things are what I do, since I don't have the freezer or counter space to make my own raw food.

—*Yogurt.* If our cat likes it, it can be a nice addition to their diet. But don't give them the heavily sugared, nonfat kind. Get the plain kind, preferably grassfed. This can be a source of probiotics and healthy fat.

Even lactose-intolerant cats enjoy it, because the process of making yogurt converts the milk sugar into substances the cat can digest.

Keeping our cats inside has wonderful effects on their safety, and safeguards our own heart. But it also means our cats are cut off from the diet they evolved to eat. I've decided the best course of action is to keep them in, and try to make it up to them in the food department.

• Better health is the gift that keeps on giving.

Grow kitty grass

Even if the cats have access to the outdoors, take care of their third major dietary need by growing them some kitty grass. I find it in the feed store. Pet supply stores, health food stores, and hardware stores who have seed sections also carry it.

This is a seed mix of tender grasses that provide living nutrients that are hard to get from processed foods. Even outdoor cats will appreciate it; greens outside could be tainted with pesticides or car exhaust, or they might have trouble finding the kind they like.

Having a tasty, clean, fresh alternative will ensure they are eating what they need, and not what they don't.

• It also means they will leave our houseplants alone.

• Wanting fresh greens is why cats bother our plants in the first place.

• We can move the cat away from our houseplants.

• Their kitty grass is a gift for them.

I keep a rotating supply of pots in the windowsill so there's always some kitty grass at the right stage. They tend not to grow perpetually, withering up at a certain stage no matter how often they are watered. That's because these are non-fruiting varieties which do not coarsen and develop seed heads. They don't last long, but will stay tender and flavorful.

We can ensure that there are good nutrients in our kitty grass by dumping a basket of used coffee grounds into the soil with each third planting. (Mix it in well.)

This will compost in place and keep our soil healthy, and we are not fertilizing with anything which could be toxic to the cat.

RJ loves his kitty grass.

Use potting soil that is formulated for indoor use, as this will keep the soil loose and let the seeds put down healthy roots. They are going to have to stand up to some tugging and chewing, since another benefit of kitty grass is the "floss" action it performs on the cat's teeth as it is being eaten.

Early on in our relationship, Mr WayofCats volunteered to plant the next pot, since we were out of seeds. He went to the hardware store and picked up a package of a brand we hadn't tried before. Our Supervisor, James Bond, viewed this change to the planting process with great skepticism, and watched over the new pot carefully.

The new kitty grass grew, and grew, and grew. When it finally withered up it was three feet long and was hanging over the pot. That's all James Bond needed to regard Mr WayofCats with new respect. *Look at that. I am impressed.*

We decided the new grass, despite its vigor, was not as tender, so we went back to the other brand. But it firmly established Mr WayofCats as a cat force to be reckoned with.

Distress signals

If the cat *doesn't eat, and this is sudden,* watch the cat's next meal choice. Try to change what we offer. If the cat consistently refuses food, this is probably a medical condition and must be checked out.

Cat moving the bowl around the kitchen. Sometimes this is because the bowl is slick, and on a slick surface. This is as annoying to the cat as it would be for us. If we see the cat moving the bowl deliberately, it means the cat would prefer a more private or easily accessible place for their bowl. See what they choose as a better spot, and see if we can accommodate them.

Cat throwing up. Cats can develop hairballs. Get some hairball remedy to help the cat, and put them on a regular schedule with it by mixing it into a meal. Look for the new "sugar free" formulations. Plant some kitty grass to soothe their stomachs.

Eating too fast. Keeping mealtimes quiet will help reassure the cat that they can take their time. There's also the trick of spreading out their canned food over an entire dinner plate. This keeps them from taking giant bites and slows them down.

Cat playing with water bowl. Leave a bowl in the tub for them to see if this satisfies. Makes it easy to rinse and refill, too.

Heal a Hungry Cat

A big food problem is when the cat never seems satisfied. Why are they constantly asking for food?

Well, they might still be hungry. They eat meat, and that's about it. Their body even makes the sugar their organs need from... protein. Fat and protein are the building blocks their body needs, and they can't use the cereal products so many cat foods are made of.

If the cat is not getting enough nutrients, they will feel hungry. Food alone doesn't turn off their appetite. Satisfaction is what turns off their appetite.

Once the cat is established with proper food, they will no longer be so quick to get hungry again. Since they aren't eating more and more in a vain attempt to satisfy their appetite, their hungry signals will calm down and be more in line with their activity level. They won't be eating cereals that can only turn into fat. They will get shiny coats and fewer digestive problems, too.

• Of course, they will still ask for food when they are hungry.

• But they won't drive us crazy asking for food all the time.

Once we have established a twice a day food schedule for the average adult cat, the cat will find they are satisfied until next time. This still leaves room for tasty treats. But the volume of the treats (unless we forget and leave them somewhere for the cat to practice their package opening skills) will not be enough to throw off their capacity for real food.

If the cat is still growing, and this phase can last up to three or four years with large breeds and their mixes, our cat will be hungry more often. So it's okay to feed them more often. With their natural diet, we don't have to worry about them overeating.

• They will be getting the proper signals.

Many of us will wind up with a cat who has food issues. Namely, lack of food. Whether we take in a stray, or rescue a cat from a shelter, chances are good this was a cat who knows what it's like to miss a meal or three. Like with humans, this situation doesn't resolve itself immediately after the meals start coming with regularity.

This is a survival issue that has sunk into the cat's brain. Our task is to get this cat to feel secure enough to stop fretting about food. This isn't a problem if we are feeding the right food. The meat diet will not cause problems for the cat's digestive system.

Mithrandir's first meal in his new forever home.

• Just feed the cat.

Nothing else will work, anyway. Cats operate on straightforward Cause and Effect. If the food isn't there, they will worry. Keeping the food coming will be the only thing that will convince the cat that the food will keep on coming.

Don't worry about them getting fat. They might, but that's okay. The extra fat, on a proper diet, will actually signal the cat that they have reached a good place. That might be the only signal the cat will listen to. They will, all by themselves, start regulating their appetite. So we don't have to.

Then their weight will go down without us being pestered all the time by a cat who feels in danger of starvation again.

Fussing about the cat getting fat, and restricting their food, will only make the problem worse. Now the cat *knows* they have a food problem, and it will be all they can think about.

With kittens, with their small tummies, we can feed a spoonful at a time, and, a few hours later, another spoonful. When I rescue starving kittens, I feed them six times a day, if need be. Once they stop being skin and bones, they will relax. And not before.

Older cats can go longer between meals. But we have to be able to trust nature, and let food be their cure.

It does work.

Slim down the fat cat

What about the chubby cat problem? Giving the cat their natural diet solves that one too.

Within six months of switching over to a proper diet, we will find most cats, no matter how chubby and lethargic they were when they started, will be slimming down. Without starving them, and without being constantly bothered to feed them.

Even a chubby cat can be constantly hungry. That's because their body can't use the food. Their body lacks the enzymes that would allow them to convert carbohydrates, that is, the grains and cereals, into actual nutrients. Cats need sugar so little that their taste buds can't even detect sweetness. All their body can do with the grains is turn them into fat.

So now we have a fat cat who is still malnourished. What can we do?

Canned food, even the cheaper brands, have far more meat in them than dry foods. This is what the cat is craving, and this is what will allow the cat to feel satisfied after eating.

So start adding canned food to the cat's routine, and start phasing out the dry foods.

Won't this be bad for the cat's teeth? No, studies show the type of food has no effect on keeping cat's teeth clean. In fact, cereal based foods can accelerate tooth decay in cats, because the cat's saliva is so bad at breaking down this kind of food. Meat tends to have more moisture in it, too, and that's important for cat health. They will automatically be getting more water in their diet from eating more canned.

Most cats love their canned, but we might have a cautious cat who isn't thrilled with change. Mix the canned into their dry food, and gradually change the proportions until they are eating mostly canned, and then only canned.

Convince the Fussy Cat

There are cats who recognize only a certain kind of food, or even a certain flavor, as food. They aren't doing it to annoy us.

Cats rely on their mothers, or their environment, to show them what is good to eat while they are growing up. Once this window of learning closes in early adolescence, many cats find accepting new food a difficult task. In the wild, this is fine, since it's unlikely a whole new species of prey will pop up for the cat to deal with.

But domestic cats who live with us can find this instinct working against them. These are cats who might have had a very restricted diet during their learning period, or were so thrilled with a certain food it becomes a favorite.

Food is such a fundamental issue it can be a difficult change for these cats. Trust is the issue here. They know what they like, and they don't want to risk not having a good meal every day.

Simply keep offering the new food, as a side dish in the same bowl with their regular food. This will open the cat's mind to the possibility. It will reassure them that this new substance is food; it's right alongside the food they prefer. This can help them at least try it.

Patience is the key. It might be annoying to us, but if it's a choice between food they like, and is bad for them, and getting them to eat at least some food that is good for them, it's a job we need to tackle.

The natural diet of cats is going to make them feel better after they eat it. Getting some of that into the cat is the vital first step to switching them over. Once they have a chance for their body to recognize the extra nutrients, the cat will start to get some pleasure from the new food, and the process will accelerate.

Cats have feedback mechanisms that are responsible for their prey drive and their very survival. The cat will allow this to "kick in" once they have a chance to get some of their natural food working in their system.

Slow and gradual change is the way to convince a cat that new food, offered long enough, can become not-so-new food. Over time, this will become, finally, safe food.

Don't be above tempting them by adding tuna juice, beef or chicken broth, or finely minced meat to make the new food more attractive while we are switching over. We won't have to do this forever, only long enough to get them over the "new food" problem.

• Eventually, the new food will no longer be new.

If we have been used to leaving a bowl of dry food out all the time, we might miss that coverage. And so might the cat.

If the cat still fusses because their buffet has been canceled, and it doesn't seem like this situation will resolve itself, there are dry foods on the market that have much more meat in them. This can be an adequate supplement to their regular diet of canned, and that can be exactly the kind of security a cat with food issues will find reassuring.

Reassure a Recovering Cat

If our cat has had an illness which caused nausea and pain, the cat can associate their distress with their food.

It's the same mechanism we find in ourselves. After getting food poisoning from a certain food, or a night out with overindulgence in a particular type of alcohol, it's very common for people to avoid that substance.

We have the benefit of being able to intellectually understand what is happening, and we still can't eat or drink that again very soon.

All the cat knows is: *that food made them sick.*

We might have to switch them to different flavors or varieties, or even some servings of people food, to get them to eat after their recovery. It's important that they eat, and at this point, it doesn't matter what. Once they have recovered, they can usually consider getting back to their favorites again.

Use the same mixing trick to reintroduce the foods back into their diet. We might have to keep trying. If the cat was very sick, that food might be off their menu for a long time.

• Giving them the right food with the right attitude makes a big difference.

Feed the Right Treats

If we have discovered that the cat was eating a poor diet, and now have switched the cat to a better one, we will often discover a new side to our cat.

Being constantly hungry makes the cat anxious. An anxious cat is going to attribute their bad feelings to their environment. They can be on edge and suspicious of even the sweetest gestures on our part.

Once the cat feels good, things will be different. Now they will attribute their good feelings to us, their home, and everything.

It's like giving them a sunny day for their mind.

If the cat had a problem with going hungry in the past, they will be even more grateful to us for solving it for them. The gratitude and love will be more obvious, and more easily given.

There's nothing wrong with feeding our cats people food. Even strange people food. I've had cats who loved marshmallows, mandarin oranges, or Cheetos. Of course, they should get such bizarre treats in tiny portions, and not too often.

If our cat will tolerate dairy, there shouldn't be any harm in these foods that have a little more nutrition. Despite their mythical attraction to milk, cats prefer cream.

A young Olwyn waiting for treats by the puzzle box.

This has more fat and fewer milk sugars, and should get along with their tummies better than milk.

Cats actually lack the ability to taste sweetness, so the sugary taste is not the attraction for them. That means if they like dairy, unsweetened yogurt would be as appealing, and better for them.

If they indicate they would like a taste of the meat on our plate, put some in their bowl. It's unlikely we are dining on raw mice, but meat has the same appeal as their natural prey.

Cats will enjoy the bits of fat or gristle that might not appeal to us. As long as they eat it without problems afterward, there's no reason why they shouldn't enjoy it.

Organ meats are also parts cats enjoy. We can pick up such parts inexpensively and simmer them into treats for the cat. Even if they aren't gravy fans, the water for poaching tastes good to them and can be another source of water.

Raw bones are another treat cats can enjoy. In the wild, cats use their sandpaper tongue to lick all the meat from the bones and get some calcium that way. Don't give them cooked bones, though, because these are brittle and no longer have the calcium in a state the cat can use.

If this process appeals to us, there are numerous recipes available for people who want to make all their own food for their cats. Properly done, this is a loving and healthful alternative. It's important to find a good recipe and follow it.

In the wild, cats eat almost all of their prey, which covers their nutritional needs. As spoiling as a diet of chicken breasts might seem, it will lack vital nutrients. Variety is more likely to cover all the bases.

All of these "treat tricks" can tempt a recovering cat to eat.

Take care of their teeth

Don't worry about feeding the cat all that canned food. Studies show that the type of food doesn't matter much when it comes to keeping their teeth clean.

- In fact, the cereal in dry food can be a contributor to cat tooth problems.

That pot of kitty grass has another benefit; it acts as "floss" for cats when they eat it.

There are cat toothbrushes on the market, with toothpaste designed to appeal to the cat's palate. Be cautious about them, and reject an ingredient list which contains *fluoride*. We can tell a small child to rinse and spit, but we can't get the cat to do it. They're going to swallow some fluoride with these toothpastes, which is not a good idea.

I've found that if we can get the cat to *enjoy chewing on the brush*, that's the important thing. Offer the brush as a toy, and see if we can get them to pounce on the business end. Their prey instincts will make them bite it, and most cats find the texture in their mouth pleasing.

- When their teeth feel better after the brush stimulation, they will start to do it on their own.

Don't try to wrestle the cat and brush their teeth for them. This will make sure they will avoid the whole idea.

It's best if they have, every few years or so, a complete cleaning, but the vet has to put them under general anesthetic, as we can imagine. So let them chew on their brush, and keep ours off limits.

Sleep problems

It's not that cats have trouble sleeping. They spend two thirds of their life sleeping in some form or another. *When* they sleep is usually where the problems occur.

Cats are dawn and dusk hunters. That's why their ability to see in the dark is so much better than ours, and why their other senses are so sharp. When things get quiet, our cat will feel more like exploring.

Establishing trust and affection with our cat will help get them into a good sleep pattern. They will then want to spend time with us when we are up, and shape their downtime behavior so it will not disturb us.

Bedtime ritual

Play with the cat until they are tired, right before bedtime. Use a wand toy or other favorite to get them leaping and running. Don't have a wand toy? (There's your problem.)

This won't get the cat charged up. We are wearing the cat out. When they start lying down and making lethargic movements, they're ready to stop. Now give them a snack, and they'll go to sleep.

Things to keep in mind

Cats do not usually sleep for many hours at a stretch. They cycle faster than that, so a few hours will get them refreshed and ready to go. However, this lands in the middle of the human's sleep cycle.

This is when we must be careful to send only the correct signals.

Things are turned down at night

It's quieter, darker, and less populated. Cats will have more confidence exploring when there are fewer inputs to deal with.

Cats miss us. The more they love us, the more they will miss when we are unavailable. When they are lonely in the middle of the night, it will be natural for them to seek us out. We must negotiate our needs and theirs. This will let us have a good night's sleep, without making the cat feel rejected.

These are principles to remember as we consider the three biggest mistakes that lead to sleep problems.

Kitten Olwyn is cute, but sleeping kittens don't stay that way long enough.

1. Creating expectations

We go to bed while it's dark and sleep all through the night. To the cat, this is very difficult to understand. Their natural inclination is to wake up at three in the morning, raring to go.

Cats need help in figuring out what we want from them.

Any cat, of any age, needs a bedtime ritual.

- We want to signal the cat when it's time for bed.

- We want to wear them out so they will naturally go to sleep.

- We want to let them know where they are expected to spend our night.

As bedtime approaches, involve the cat in the process. Talk to them as we do our turning out the lights thing, the shutting the off television thing, the washing up thing. Whatever we do to get ready for bed each night, we need to involve the cat as much as they are able.

A kitten will naturally have a shorter attention span than an adult, but each time we start our bedtime ritual, they will learn more.

If the cat is playful during the day, start a play session as part of bedtime.

- Don't worry about getting the cat charged up.

- This is ramping the cat down.

Cats don't have energy longevity. A good play session before bed will tire them out. It also acts as a signal that it's perfectly all right for them to seek out a quiet place when they are tired, one where they will not be disturbed.

Cats will find a good place to sleep. They will find many good places to sleep. Like us, they prefer their different sleeping spots to be roomy, quiet, and cushy.

So don't think we can keep the cat off the furniture.

They might like to stretch out on a rug, especially if there's a patch of sunlight they can follow on it, but they will also love to sleep in chairs, on couches, and our bed.

It's a way of being close to us, and breathe in our scent.

2. Consistent Signals

We want the cat to cuddle with us, but we don't want them interfering with our sleep.

We have to know what we want before we start trying to train the cat towards it.

• An important early decision is where the cat will sleep when we are sleeping too.

I've taken the easiest path. They sleep with us, and the bedroom door is open.

If this is possible, it solves many problems at once. The cat can come and go as they please, hitting the litter or food bowls as needed. It's that fast cycling. Cats are not going to conk out for eight hours at a stretch.

If our cats love us, they want to be with us. That includes the bedroom. If we are quiet, in a dark room, they will take our cues from us and come in for sleeping with us on the bed. When they are awake, they will leave the room to do other things, and come back again when they are sleepy.

The cat, before they learn sleep manners, will be up, and want us to be up too. To convince the cat we are sleeping, even if we are not, we have to *do nothing*.

• Once the cat learns that **Sleep Mode** means we are not available, they will leave us alone to sleep.

But before they learn that, they will try to get us up to play with them, feed them, and pet them. We don't do this in Sleep Mode. We do nothing.

242

So if the cat paws at our face, calls to us, or walks on our head, the right thing to do is nothing.

• Not reacting to the cat's efforts is essential.

How is the cat going to know that sleep means we are unavailable… if the cat does something… and we make ourselves available?

Cats are all about Cause and Effect. They know the first step is to get our attention. If we notice their efforts to get our attention, the cat regards that as a success.

The cat will not find our getting up grumpy to be a failure. They don't think that way. Their goal was to get us up. We might not feel that way, but the best way to convey this attitude to the cat is thwart them at the outset. No matter what the cat does, while we are either sleeping or supposed to be sleeping, we must do nothing.

• We cannot convince them, once we are awake and reacting to them, that we don't want to be awake and reacting to them.

That's because the cat operates from their own principles. One of the biggest is: They only do things they *want* to do.

They think humans, who are after all more capable than they are in the world we both live in, are the same way. We operate the can opener. We make food appear and ugly litter clumps disappear. We are so powerful, we can't possibly do anything we don't want to do.

• If we are up, it's *because* we responded to the cat's invitation.

They think that's all they are doing; inviting us to take advantage of this invitation to do something with them. If we do it, it must be because we *wanted* to do it.

• If we don't want to be awake at this time, we aren't awake.

• It's that simple, and that difficult.

The only way to convince the cat we don't want to be awake while we are in Sleep Mode is to pretend, with all our might, that we are always asleep when it is time for sleeping.

If the cat does not get the reaction they wanted, they will conclude that we cannot be gotten out of sleep as easily as they can. So they will find other things to do, and come back on the bed when they want to sleep, too.

Why shouldn't they? The bed is comfy and quiet and we are lying there, looking like we are asking for a cat to curl up in the curve of our knees, against our feet, or cuddle up against our chest. Affectionate cats won't pass up this opportunity.

3. Flag a pit stop

There are times when we have to get up, such as calls of nature. Don't be surprised if the cat lights up and starts trying to interact with us. *Yay. We're up.*

Once again, the only way to convince the cat we are not really up is to take care of business and go right back to bed. The cat must learn that even if we visit our litter in the middle of the night, we still don't want to be up.

So we must ignore the cat. Ignore the cat's entreaties once we are back in bed. If we keep this up successfully, the cat will realize *Sleep Mode is powerful.*

- Sleep Mode operates even if it seems like we are getting up, but then go right back to bed.

Help the cat to this conclusion by making our trips quick and to the point, and offer cues that are not part of our normal waking up process. Keep lights off and side activity for the morning.

Don't go in the kitchen. This will set the cat's breakfast process in motion, and it will be our fault. We can't, to the cat, make an offer and then not deliver on it.

It's different if we want a snack. Turn on the lights, and settle down for a while. Now we are Up, and can be with our cat.

Deal with the 3 AM Problem

We might get to sleep fine, and so does the cat. But then the cat wakes up, misses us, and starts howling and scratching at the bedroom door. Chances are, if we have this problem, we have already trained the cat. Now we have to retrain the cat.

It's probable that when this happened, we said something to the cat, opened the door to shoo the cat away, or otherwise reacted to the cat's attempts to get attention.

- This is how we train the cat to *do this more*.

- They are getting a *reaction*.

- So, how do we *retrain* the cat?

We give them something to do. Create a "depths of the night" toy box or other quiet distraction that we put out in the living room when we go to bed. This contains things they like but will only be available to them at night. Explain that this is for playing with while we are still sleeping.

If we could have it opened by them as needed or by some remote method, all the better.

When we put the toy box away in the morning, they will soon realize these toys are only available during our sleeping cycle, and they will be more eager to play with them while they can.

They have to see that they are not getting us up at 3 AM, but we are still meeting their needs at such times. Of course, the toys and treats must be quiet; no balls with bells in them. But anything that engages their minds (*how do we get the toybox open?*) will keep them from being bored.

We are not trying to mess up our relationship. We are simply letting them know they must come up with their own amusements when we are needing privacy and quiet in the bedroom.

Sleep time signals

We have to remember cats have fast sleep cycles. So our being away from them all night is like our being away for two days.

What signals are the cats giving us about their nighttime options? How can we address these needs the cats are signaling?

—*Bedtime arrives too abruptly.* If the cat looks around and we are gone, this can trigger separation anxiety. They are not anticipating, and so they are not mentally prepared for us to vanish.

Do give them a few rounds of *okay, here you go* cuddling before we try to get some sleep. This is their cuddle time, when we are down and helpless, and they plan to take full advantage. They can look forward to this part of the day when we plan for it.

If the cat is sleeping at our bedtime, pet them lightly and say goodnight to them. That way, they won't wake up and wonder if we have vanished.

—*Cat wants affection.* If the cat wakes us up by rubbing their head on us, purring, or flopping down beside us, respond with a soft word or some petting while we are still in Sleep Mode. If we aren't sure that is what the cat wants, grab them and pull them into a big hug.

• If that's what they want, they will relax and go to sleep.

• If that's not what they want, they will avoid us when we are sleeping.

This is an excellent way of not rejecting the cat, and still getting sleep. How can the cat be upset with us when we want to hug them when we are in our Sleep Mode? So if the cat is trying to get us up for some other purpose, they will be thwarted.

—*Noisy nighttime activity.* The cat can take our unavailability to heart, and find ways to amuse themselves at night. But what if these are noisy ways?

Get some quiet toys that will be only for nighttime. Put some treats in an empty tissue box, the kind with the plastic window, and let them figure out how to get them. Pick up those balls with bells in them before bed. Or we will be hearing them later.

—*Signal it's bedtime.* Make a point of involving them in our go-to-bed rituals. Making the cat a part of our bedtime lets them know what is about to happen. They won't mind our "leaving" them so much if we have paid attention to them beforehand.

—*Wear them out.* Cats can be worn out with some active playing with a wand toy or ball toss. Making their playtime a part of our bedtime makes it more likely they will be tired, too. With kittens, and their extra energy, it's important we help them burn it off.

- Play until the cat starts lying down to make their moves.

- This is a sign they are feeling tired.

—*Bedtime can be cuddle time.* One technique is to make it clear to the cat that this is a good time to get some cuddling, prior to us going to sleep. Bring them into the bedroom with us, or call them when we are settled down.

Cats adore affection offered when we are on their level. Lying down in bed transforms us. We are no longer a towering figure with a face far over their head. We are now an interactive face they can approach as an equal.

This is why cats so often bother us at bedtime. It is actually a compliment, and we should treat it as such. It's a great way to create an affectionate cat.

Scratching, explained

I know it might seem that we adopted a cat and gotten a free shredding machine. How did this overwhelm us?

That's because cats will use their litter box, eat, and sleep; all without training. We might not have the best situation in the world, but we do have a situation that works adequately for most cats, most of the time. So a lot of homes muddle along without a human needing to know how to train a cat.

That doesn't happen with scratching behavior.

To make matters worse, cats seem driven to scratch in the worst of all possible places, resulting in the partial or wholesale destruction of expensive objects which are difficult to fix. So the action many people feel driven to take when confronted with scratching problems is even more horrible than litter box problems putting a cat in the shelter.

That would be: declawing.

• See page 259: Declawing creates a crazy cat

It's a shame and a pity; because with the right approach, and the right equipment, it's really easy to train a cat where and what to scratch.

—*What to Do Right Away:* Usually, there's one room and one place that is the cat's favorite. Take their scratching post and fasten it over that surface. Use rope, duct tape, or whatever will fix the post firmly in place without damage, because this won't be a permanent solution, but a retraining tool.

Don't have a scratching post? (There's your problem.) A cardboard box, folded over to have at least two layers, can be fastened over the area. We can use this in any places which need protection.

Things to keep in mind

We must remember that this is a *survival issue*.
The cat's instincts demand that they:

- "Sharpen" their claws by pulling off old claw sheaths.

- Stretch and strengthen their body.

- Send signals to other cats.

- Release nervous tension.

- Mark their home as theirs.

- Show excitement and happiness.

So we can see that scratching behavior has a multitude of uses, and covers a lot of the cat's needs.

- Scratching problems get so bad because of the **Spiral of Desperation**.

The cat has to scratch for a lot of reasons; including stress relief. We start the process by getting the wrong scratching post. (It's not entirely our fault; most scratching posts are wrong.) The cat sensibly chooses a better alternative, and we yell at them for it.

The cat, confused by getting yelled at for something that is as essential as breathing, gets stressed, and scratches more. We escalate by squirting them with water, or even hitting them. The cat, now even more stressed, scratches more.

And so on.

We must start over, as it were, from scratch.

- We block off whatever the cat shouldn't be scratching.

- We start offering proper substitutes.

• We start over with the training, skipping the yelling and other angry methods.

Commit to these three steps, and we'll see where we went wrong, because the cat is totally blameless about what and where they scratch.

Wrong scratching post

Cat paws are marvels of engineering. Cats actually walk on their toes, and the retractable claws are hidden to keep them sharp and also to not betray their stealthy approach to prey. Claws are one of the cat's special hunting tools, and so they will devote a certain amount of their time to their maintenance.

Cats are sharpening their claws when they scratch things, but not in the way we might think. Cat's claws actually consist of many nested sheaths, one inside the other. New sheaths are constantly being produced from the inside, and the cat pulls off the old, dull sheaths from the outside.

It's like those inexpensive plastic pencils which have a number of short leads in little cones stacked up in the pencil. One lead gets dull, and we pull off that cone and place it in the back of the pencil, pushing a sharp lead into place for writing.

When they need to scratch, and they will, cats look for something to combine their needs for a yielding surface on a sturdy base.

• It's not their fault furniture is the best thing around.

If we had some trees around the house, both upright and fallen, we would have perfect scratching posts. Since that is what cats would look for, we should apply, to any potential scratching post, the **Trees Test**. How much is this scratching post like a tree?

Without the Trees Test, we will buy the flimsy, the clumsy, and the abrasive scratching posts, and wonder why the cat won't use them.

Cats need something soft for tender paw pads, something yielding so they can vary their pull, and something sturdy, so they can really get their backs into it.

• Imagine using a Bowflex held together with paperclips, and we can see why bad scratching posts are avoided.

• Any post that swings or drags too easily is more annoying than useful.

• If they can't dig their claws in, if it won't handle their weight, it will not satisfy all their urges.

Mithy demonstrates a scratcher with sturdiness and a surface cats can sink their claws into.

A cat who is wound up from activity will often head for their scratching places to burn off some of that exuberance, and to use that energy to scratch higher and deeper than before. Cats use their scratch marks to let other cats know whose territory this is, and also how big and strong they are. That's why cats need sturdy items to scratch, so they can dig in and exercise their whole body.

So while their favorite furniture is blocked off, try to duplicate what it is that attracts them, so we can come up with an adequate substitute.

• The best, and easiest, way to keep cats from scratching our furniture is to give them their own stuff that they like better.

Cats needing to be relocated from the corner of the couch are asking for an upholstered, tall scratching post with a broad sturdy base. Cats who scratch on the throw rugs or carpet want large flat surfaces.

• We must invest in a good piece of cat furniture

• Or offer a cheap, but slightly messy, substitute

This handy substitute can be the Alpine line of upright or flat cat scratchers made from cardboard. The cat's body weight helps hold it in place, and cats love the texture of the cardboard scratching surfaces.

• We can get something that does not have much mass, but we can fasten it to something that does.

Try different textures in toys or cheaper devices until we can tell if the cat likes it or not. If they like rope-wrapped toys, they would probably like that texture in a scratching post.

It has to be able to stand up to our cat's body weight, so we can fasten it to something stationary and get more bulk easily. Secure a good but insubstantial type of scratching post to some more sturdy object as a way of getting more stability for the cat.

• This can be the best route to resolving a space or money difficulty when we cannot invest in cat furniture.

It doesn't matter what kind of scratching post we get as long as we come up with something the cat likes. That must be the criteria.

• No matter how much *we* like it, the cats must make their own decisions.

Make sure the scratching posts are oriented properly for the cat's use.

• Some cats like to scratch while they stretch their bodies OUT, so there should be a vertical part.

• Some cats like to stretch UP, and they need a vertical part.

• Some like BOTH.

Furniture for the cat can be an attractive option, if chosen properly. Most cats love it, but the design must suit them in a few ways. It has to be secure for climbing on, have the right kind of surface, and have an open design that is accessible to the athletic ability of the targeted cats.

The elongated Foreign types are the most likely to enjoy the more complicated cat structures. The stockier, broad-headed cobby types can leap and climb, but would enjoy more straightforward arrangements, such as a design with stairsteps or ramps.

Closepiled, dense carpets, like Berber, are cat favorites. Avoid extremes like shag (not enough substance,) or indoor/outdoor, (not enough depth,) which lack appealing textures.

• Cats want to SINK their claws into their scratching post.

So invest some time before the money, and do some research, both on available options, and on what surface and stability each cat likes.

This will keep us from saying, as many do, "I spent oodles of money on that, and the cat ignores it."

See what the cat likes, and *then* get them something they like.

Wrong place

Cats also use their scratching behaviors to mark territory as theirs, and show off how big and strong they are.

We need scratching posts where we spend time, which should also be where the cats spend time. Don't put the scratching post in the basement and expect the cat to use it. They don't "go somewhere" to scratch the way they "go somewhere" to use the bathroom.

The point of scratching is that cats do it in their places to hang out. It's part of their hanging out. Cats are not capable of handling their stress anxieties by any lack of action. They need stress relief and territory signals in their territory.

Territorial issues, badly handled, can add to a cat's stress, and then make them want to scratch more, in more places, in an attempt to feel at home.

These same territorial instincts can be used to our advantage by giving them scratching posts in handy places. Handy for the cat; handy for us to put the cat on while retraining.

• Teach the cat their scratching post is theirs by putting them on it every time we see them scratching something they shouldn't.

• Make it appealing by making a big fuss over it being *for them*.

• Use one of our Way of Cats Herbal Blends to make it more attractive to our cat's senses.

Often, cats will be excited by seeing us come back home and want to scratch something. This is a perfect time to carry them over to their scratching post and make a fuss over them using it.

When frustrated from being redirected from our furniture, cats are in the perfect mood to find something they can scratch that will please us.

• Have that perfect thing handy, and half our training is done for us.

So give the cat some leeway in choosing the places where they will be most comfortable. They pick these places for many reasons, but one of them is about us. They want to be near us, see what we are doing, get some interaction going. Any place we spend time in should have a cat's place too. Their insistence in such matters is a compliment, and should be respected.

Watch the reinforcement

We create a bad cat relationship when we make the cat want to avoid us. Scratching behaviors happen right in front of us for a reason.

The cat isn't trying to be "bad" or annoy us. They are expressing their happiness and joy, and many times that comes out in an irresistible impulse to scratch something.

If all they have to scratch is things they aren't supposed to scratch, we have set up a Spiral of Desperation; the cat goes to scratch something, we yell at them, they avoid us, and stuff gets scratched, anyway.

So we must respond properly when they scratch things; good or bad. The steps to redirect cats to a scratching post we know they like are these:

• Take the cat away from the wrong scratching spot, and take them to the scratching post they like. They will usually transfer their scratching to the post. Now praise with excitement.

• If we see them scratching something they shouldn't, we don't yell or get angry. We act sad, tell them to leave that alone, and if they don't run to their scratching post, take them there.

• We have to show the cat what we want them to do instead of scratching the furniture, because telling them to leave the furniture alone will not meet their needs.

• Use a squirt bottle or blast of canned air *on the wrong spot* to make the spot less appealing.

• We can also put aluminum foil, plastic wrap, or double sided sticky tape on the spot, or block it off for a while. If the cat can't get at it, they can't get pleasurable feedback from scratching it, and will then lose the urge.

• Be patient with kittens, who will often scratch the nearest object out of excitement when we play or talk to them. Pick them up and take them to their post.

Declawing creates a crazy cat

It's outright cruel to declaw the cat. It's senseless, too.

It eliminates the scratching by taking away what the cat does it with. But it doesn't take away the cat's needs. And now we've created a much more stressful situation for the cat.

There isn't any way of taking the claws away that does not cripple the cat's feet. Hold out your hand. Imagine having the first joint of the fingers cut off. That's what declawing does. While this would harm our piano playing and typing, it would also harm our walking. Cats walk on their toes.

So now we've created a crippled cat who cannot burn off energy by scratching, and they also cannot burn off energy by running around. Even if the cat heals quickly, they are no longer the cat they once were.

Cats often don't heal quickly. At least a third of declawing operations lead to complications, infections, and further surgery.

All of this creates a cat with body problems they can't solve. Even if the cat is not in constant pain from its mutilated paws, it is in constant pain because they cannot walk and run and exercise the way they should. This creates more health problems.

We no longer have a pet. We have a sick, neurotic cat who has trouble giving and receiving affection. Who doesn't scratch a couch but will tend to bite.

So do yourself, and the cat, a favor. If we think the only way we can keep the cat is to have it declawed, we should STOP. And take the cat to a no-kill shelter.

A whole cat, with easily retrainable problems, has a much better shot at a new home than the sick, distressed, and crippled cat we will create by declawing.

Such a cat has no shot at all.

I am not exaggerating.

The Petfinder tool shows cats up for adoption. Try it in your browser.

The damning paw, symbol of a declawed cat, is rarely alone. We will also see the symbols for "no kids, no other cats, no dogs". This is a cat with problems. They can't get along with others easily. They don't have good pet prospects.

• That's why declawed cats show up in shelters in much higher numbers than they represent in the pet population.

Every Petfinder purple paw symbolizes a cat crippled by someone who paid money to have this done, thinking it would make the cat a better pet.

It was supposed to keep this cat in their home.

Why, then, does this cat not have one?

Create grooming times

We can take care of them, and help them with their scratching training, by establishing a grooming routine together.

• Scratching and grooming are connected in the cat's mind.

Often, after a grooming session, they will head for their scratching post, and we are right there to direct them properly, and fuss over them for being good cats.

Humans will use grooming behaviors when they are nervous; smoothing or twisting their hair, inspecting their nails, plucking imaginary lint on their pants. So do cats. "When in doubt, wash," has long been a cat motto.

This self-soothing behavior is a way for them to get time to think, to feel a sense of control, and to feel good about themselves after they failed to negotiate a tricky maneuver.

This insistence on having every hair in its proper place means good ways of petting the cat all involve not disarranging their fur. Don't pet against the natural lie of the fur, don't squash their ears down, and don't rumple the cat.

• Careless petting will not communicate affection, and what else is petting for?

Cats groom themselves to keep them invisible to the noses of their potential prey. But we have a great side benefit in that the cat is usually clean, tidy, and easy to cuddle.

Brushing and combing the cat is a service we can provide, and cats will enjoy it when properly motivated. This keeps the fur shedding down and can be a delightful bonding opportunity. Brushes work well with shorthaired cats, and combs work better on the longer haired varieties.

• Cats with long, fine fur will outright need combing, since they will have a much greater tendency to mat, and they can't handle it themselves.

Mithrandir's feral side didn't let us keep him groomed during a growth spurt where he got the nickname, "The Sheep". We had to get him a lion cut to get the mats out. Now, he lets us keep him groomed.

Longhaired natural breeds, like the Main Coon Cat and the Norwegian Forest Cat, have lessened tendencies to mat, despite their long fur. Their finest fur is distributed among the coarser guard hairs that protect them from harsh weather, so if we want a longhaired cat but not a constant grooming schedule, they are a good choice.

• Grooming does more than reduce shedding and hairballs.

• Grooming lets the cat get used to human contact, by persuading them with a feel-good reward that is built into the process.

• If our cat is hand shy, or skittish about contact, a consistent grooming schedule is a way to connect with the cat, and direct their scratching behavior.

• If the cat is used to being handled, it's easy to pick up the cat and move them to where their scratching post is.

—*Start slow.* Kittens will regard it as a game, adults will regard it as an intrusion. They will learn to see the fun in our approach with comb (longhairs) or brush (shorthairs). Start with a few strokes along the back, like petting, and with adults, try the back of the neck and then a face touch up. Follow with a treat. Let them wrestle with the tool at first. Later, when they learn to enjoy it for its own sake, they will stop doing that.

—*Don't push.* This isn't a task to be completed. Grooming stimulates the cat and they can get rowdy. If this happens, stop. It's time for a treat. As the cat learns to relax and enjoy the petting aspect, we can cover more territory in a grooming session.

Once the cat enjoys the grooming, don't start with the face. Start with the tail, and work our way towards the face, which is their favorite part to be groomed. This way they learn to wait for their favorite part, and have more tolerance for touchy areas like hindquarters and belly.

• If they bail midway, let them.

• Come back the next day to go over the missed parts.

• Remember, *fun.*

They will probably want the treat anyway, but get some token grooming strokes in before we give it to them. Otherwise, they will never get around to the grooming part.

Take this opportunity to check their ears, their paws, and their teeth. They will put up with it for the reward they know is coming, which is the face fussing as much as the treat.

• Enjoy it. Get some petting and ear rubbing and affection in, and make it part of the grooming ritual.

Don't be offended if they go off and do touchups on our handiwork. This is part of coming down from the stimulation of the grooming, which cranks the cat up.

Grooming isn't always about keeping the cat looking good, since most of them feel they are quite capable of that, thank you. Grooming is a way to connect with the cat and take care of them.

So approach this with love, and they will respond.

In or Out

—*Should we let our cat out?* I always lean towards No.

—*Don't they want to go out?* Of course they do. But they only know the fun, not the dangers.

For every cat who lives to a ripe old age without incident, there are dozens of cats who do not. When I was new to cats, I didn't know any better; I let them out. My first cat, a stray I took in, got lost when I moved, and let her out too early.

• Keep our cats in at least three weeks after a move, to reset their homing routines.

The next one was still a kitten when he was hit by a car. I decided this was a risk I would no longer take.

Not their wild

While cats still have a full set of wild instincts, this does not equip them for the modern outdoors. The qualities that make our cats better pets actually work against them in the wild. Being tamed has played up their relaxed, mellow, side. That is not the side they need outdoors.

It's the nervous, suspicious, downright-anti-social cats who would fare best as solitary wilderness hunters. That is how cats "go feral" and gain a wary edge. Because there are predators out there, and some of them are human.

Unless our cat was raised as a feral, they would not have learned the adjunct skills their mother would have taught them. They still don't cope that well. The life expectancy of an unsupported feral cat is only about two or three years. If our cat encounters a feral in their territory, it can lead to fights.

Cats have strategies that help them outwit or outrun their enemies. But they cannot do that with cars and trucks. Outside cats are always getting trapped because they curled up in a place that, in nature, would not change. But now a box has closed or a door has shut and they are unable to get out.

Our cats are no longer equipped to survive in the wild, any more than we are.

The lake would be an irresistible lure, encouraging Tristan to cross the busy road.

Assess the risks

A busy road right outside our house is an excellent reason to make our cats indoor-only. Many parts of the US have coyotes which roam in packs. The forests near my home contain the giant weasels known as fishers which are equally dangerous to cats.

Even the middle ground of a quiet suburban street has trucks and off-leash dogs and puddles of antifreeze. Our cats have adaptive reflexes, but very few of them still live in the environment where these survival instincts are at their most useful.

Gamma cats are the breeds furthest from their natural instincts, but this will keep them drowsing on the picnic table, out of most harm's way. Our Beta's social outreach could get them easily picked up by a person who does not have a friendly motive. Our Alpha cats are going to look for trouble, and then be more likely to get into some.

Dogs at least have collars, while a cat's has to be a *break-away type*, or they can get trapped by it. Microchipping is a better idea whether we let them out, or not, because accidents happen.

Another innovation is to put an orange collar on our indoor cats, so that if they are seen outdoors, they are spotted as an "escapee".

Outdoors, safely

One alternative is to leash-train them. One of my friends adopted a cat from a shelter who pined for the outdoors. The compromise was a harness and leash, with shade and water available, and her cat was content to sun herself on the picnic table, which could be seen from indoors.

Other cats will stay inside a clearly defined yard. Usually. I prefer things like catios, which I once built myself out of chain link dog kennel panels. This gave them the outdoors without the hazards of getting lost or attacked by irate homeowners. Recently cats have come under fire as bird-killers, even though humans are the ones destroying habitat and using pesticides, which are far more dangerous to birds.

I am personally astonished that in an age where more cats than ever are being kept indoors, cats are being targeted as the cause of bird depopulation. If anything, cats also protect birds, by hunting the rats who eat bird eggs.

But if we do try these safer outdoor alternatives, be aware that we will need to manage fleas and ticks, and discuss a more rigorous vaccination schedule with our veterinarian. With my cats indoor only, I can stretch out vaccinations over years, since their chance of exposure is so low.

• Yearly vaccinations have been shown to be more hazardous than helpful.

As with everything we do for our cats, we sometimes need to make decisions for them, using our greater human knowledge.

What happened to Reverend Jim?

Did he make a complete recovery?

I am happy to say humans and cats worked together to help RJ make it *all the way back*.

With all his Maine Coon Cat genes on full display, he is our Gentle Giant.

He is now everything a cat should be, and the happy heart of our home.

Reverend Jim is one of the many kittens and cats out there, gems for the rescuing. My mission will never end until they all have homes.

It begins again with this book, and with you.

"The reason Heaven and Earth can last forever
Is that they do not exist for themselves
Thus they can last forever."

— Chapter 7, *The Tao Te Ching*

Glossary

Affection Moves - the many ways of letting our cat know we love them, from simple to elaborate. Page 5

Big Giant Head - interact with only our head, and hands behind our back, to be less intimidating. Page 81

Bless the Spot - telling a cat that this spot, where they are now, is fine with us. Page 14

Body Language - a cat's native language uses posture and expression instead of words. Page 9

Bond of Trust - what creates our cat friendship and lets us trade favors. Page 74

Cat Alerts - explaining an upcoming event that will happen so the cat won't be surprised. Page 96

Cat Appreciator - cat fan, cat lover, cat person. Page 2

Cat Database - the cat's memory storage system, sorted by emotional weight. Page 31

Cat Etiquette - ways of being polite and showing regard to our cats. Page 35

Cat Explanations - the cat's ability to gain meaning from our best Catspeak, which gets better when both of us practice. Page 92

Cat Fearful - a person who displays a fear of cats. Page 37

Cat Kisses - the way to smile in Catspeak. Page 21

Cat Poker - the cat game of taking turns missing one another, and seeking each other out. Page 155

Cat Potential - who the cat could be if they max out their possibilities. Page 126

Cat Radio - the constant signals our cat sends with their behavior and body language. Page 28

Cat Routines - helps cats make sense of their environment. It is a way of exercising their hunting instincts of anticipation and participation. Page 90

Cat Skeptic - someone prejudiced against cats. Page 2

Cat Types - three Cat Types with different needs and benefits. Page 125

Cats are Lawyers - cats have enough intelligence to interpret the rules and find loopholes. Page 62

Outpost - designated area where a cat is welcome to be, which keeps them out of trouble. Page 13

Paw of Compassion - our cat's way of expressing sympathy when we are upset, often with their paw laid on our arm. Page 121

Paw Play - when we treat our cat's paws like a human hand. Page 109

Perspective Tricks - approaching our cat in ways which suggest we are the same size. Page 78

Pet With Our Voice - expressing emotion with our voice to show affection to our cat. Page 21

Petting In Place - pet the cat while they stay where they are, to show respect by not rearranging them from their carefully chosen posture. Page 35

Pick a Spot - this tells our cat they should choose an Outpost to hang out in, letting them be a companion without getting into trouble. Page 101

Positive Discipline - we use guidance, not punishment, to ask the cat for what we want. Page 11

Presence - credit for simply showing up because cats regard their presence as a gift. Page 157

Red Flare of Distress - misbehavior with the purpose of telling us about our cat's distress. Page 185

Redirection - responding to misbehavior by giving cat energy an outlet which pleases us both. Page 12

Secret Hand - a training game which helps a cat get over their fear of hands. Page 105

Security Object - a fabric toy or cat blanket which we can rub on the back of our neck to imprint with our scent. Page 59

Shaping the Response - guiding our cat towards a conclusion with the help of our own emotional input. Page 86

Show Me - a training game where the cat learns to show us what they want. Page 26

Sleep Mode - a training technique where once we are "asleep" we can't respond, even if we get up for a bathroom trip or to check on something. Page 242

Spiral of Desperation - the situation where the cat expresses a need, the human tries to punish them out of it, the cat does it more out of desperation, the human punishes more from frustration, and no one is being each other's friend. Page 249

Subtitling - a way of combining cat (body) language with human language, which translates for our cat. Page 20

Supervisor - cat who loves to be with us and monitor our activities. Page 100

The Shift - passively staying flat on the floor and letting them pick a body part to exchange affection with. Page 79

Their Origin Story - show affection by telling our cat how we found them. Page 162

Thing We Can't Ignore - when the cat trains us by deliberately doing something we must respond to. Page 47

Tortitude - female-linked tri-color coats might indicate a certain Bossiness. Page 132

Toy Rotation - putting away toys our cat is bored with, and bringing in "new" toys that were put away. Page 39

Train With Drama - by using clearly expressed emotion, in body language and voice tones, to get our meaning across to our cat. Page 50

Trees Test - in nature our cats would scratch on sturdy trees with bark they can sink their claws into, so look for these kinds of scratching posts. Page 251

Trust Games - the right kind of teasing that lets our cat know we are playing. Page 107

Villain Hands - a training game which lets us slowly approach a cat and withdraw before they get too nervous. Page 106

Volume Control - acknowledging our cat's acute senses and not overloading them by being loud or threatening. Page 21

World They Did Not Make - our cats have wild instincts that they adapt to our human world. Page 16

Yours and Mine - redirect our cat's energy towards something even better, and they leave our stuff alone. Page 54

About the Author

Pamela Merritt has been rescuing kittens and cats for decades. This is how she developed her special techniques for healing trauma, figuring out the different Types of cats, and then matching them with Forever Homes.

Seen here with her latest rescue, recovering feral Mithrandir, on the day of his adoption

She enjoys the support of Cat Appreciators all over the world through her popular blog, at the WayofCats.com website.

She has combined her honors degree in human psychology with her decades of experience in amateur cat rescue to develop the *Way of Cats*.

This is a unique Cat Management System which is based on mutual understanding, communication, and affection.

This volume is the first in a series which will apply the *Way of Cats* to such topics as kitten raising, multiple cats, cat training, special cat care, and how to get maximum affection.

She is available for *Cat Consultations* via video or phone.
It is all part of a simple, yet profound, mission:

More cats in more homes.

Reviews

United States:

5.0 out of 5 stars

*****Magical; the cat book you've been missing.

You need a cat manual. This one is magical. This is the cat manual you & your cat need and deserve. Pamela Merritt knows how to relate to cats. She has the gift of being able to see how their minds work, and it's not hard to learn - but if you're like me you're probably going to need to have it illustrated for you, to get you started. I have explained Pamela's insight & tips to several cat parents and they have all gotten this look of relief, happiness, and confidence that they can enjoy and work with their cats with success and mutual understanding after hearing them. This is more than just a "manual," too. If you read and take these ideas to heart, you will begin to have such a deeper and more rewarding - yes, magical! - relationship with your cats, too. We who love cats do so partly due to their intelligence & the human-like "relationship of equals" we get to share with them. This book expands on that very special premise and relationship quality, taking the best part of cat-human relationships and opening it up like a flower.

***** Helped me considerably with my own cats! Amazing insights.

I started reading the author's blog a couple months ago -- I came for the cat stories, and stayed for the cat psychology. She explained a lot about the behavior of my two cats that I didn't understand or realize--we all had a good relationship, but she made it even better. When we decided to add another cat to the family, I read all of her posts on how to choose a cat, and, using that advice, we were able to choose a cat who is a major sweetie, and is starting to fit in with the others.

So I couldn't wait to get this book, and it is everything I hoped for: more cat stories and more insights! She has an easy writing style, but don't mistake that for lack of depth, or 'wishful thinking' about what cats are like. She knows her stuff, and, yes, she brings considerable experience, but what is even more important is that she brings the right kind of scientific imagination to understand cat cause and effect.

I hope there is a hand-held version in the future, because I can this becoming my go-to gift for new cat owners, or, really, any cat owners. In fact, anyone interested in animal psychology!

***** So helpful! Better than Jackson Galaxy!

Way of Cats is the most helpful cat advice I've ever come across. After discovering the blog years ago, I started using the techniques to improve my relationship with my old cat. By the time he passed, we had a relationship so solid even chronic illness, twice daily medications and regular baths didn't phase him (he wasn't happy about any of it, but he understood that I had to do all of it for his own good). I read this book a few months after he passed, in preparation for bringing a pair of new kitties home (just in case he was a fluke, and as a refresher since he was my only cat for 15 years). So far, so good! They scratch their scratching posts, they seem to trust us and more or less listen when I tell them no (the actual dangerous stuff they grasped right away, it's just things like staying off the coffee table they don't seem to understand yet). I'm even working on slowly introducing them to healthier food and the supplements mentioned, and so far little to no digestive upset seems to be happening. And the advice for how to approach a skittish cat (or just a cat who doesn't know you yet) has been invaluable for my volunteer work with a local shelter. If you want a better relationship with your cats, I definitely recommend this book (or at least check out the blog).

***** **There is plenty in here for novice and expert alike!**

have been a cat guardian for 20 years, and still feel that there were many great insights in this book to help understand these little felines better. My husband, a self-proclaimed dog person, has struggled to understand the way of cats. I've insisted that he read this book, and recommend the same for those that struggle to bond with cats. I already see that some of the advice is helping him. I highly recommend the book, and hope there is a print version in the future. Would love to gift this to lots of friends and family.

***** **This is such a good insight about cats.**

Man, I wish I'd had this book 20 years ago. I've had lots of cats all my life, but this author put more into one book than everything I ever learned, tripled. For anybody who really loves cats and wants a good relationship with them, this is the best book ever. I'm going to buy my two favorite "cat ladies" this book for Christmas. :-)

***** **Excellent understanding of cats.**

I've followed Pam's blog for a few years and this book is a wonderful distillation of her ideas and experience. She gives clear examples of putting her philosophy in action. I've picked up several new ideas that I'm trying out with my cats already!

Pam has great advice not only for those of us with cats, but also for people looking to get a new cat.

***** **A how-to guide for cat owners.**

A lot of great information on interacting with our feline companions! Entertaining read from the Way of Cats blogger!

***** **This was a fun, quick read.**

I have been a cat mom for almost 10 years but this taught me a lot about my cat's language and needs. I really enjoyed this as my first kindle unlimited read.

***** If your cat does anything you'd rather it not do, you need this book

This book has helped me understand cats so much. For example, I can now safely cook in the kitchen while my cat supervises from his spot instead of getting underfoot. It's like magic, but it's in this book! Thanks to her advice, none of our furniture is scratched.

***** If you live with a cat, you should read this book!

This is an excellent book to teach you how to communicate with your cat so your cat understands you, and you understand your cat! A wonderful book, and one I recommend to any cat owner, even those of us who've had cats all our lives.

***** Extremely knowledgeable author!

This woman knows what she's doing! I have learned so so much about communicating with my cats and reading the way they communicate with me. It's knowledge I have passed on to other cat lovers countless times. Her understanding of our feline companions has been so valuable! If you buy only one book to help you understand cats, it should be this one.

***** Real solutions to cat problems, can't recommend highly enough!

I've relied on Pam's blog for years now, and it is so nice to have it all organized in one place. I've had cats for 44 years, and still learned so much from her.

***** Practical Help!

Pamela Merritt has helped better understand each of my cat's personality and special needs to make them (and myself) happier.

Canada:

5.0 out of 5 stars

***** **Your cat will love you more for reading this book!**
Pamela Merritt has taught me so much about how to improve my relationship with my cat, and we are both thankful to her!! I first found her help through her blog, and when her book became available I snapped it up. It is full of good information and even the ideas I first rolled my eyes at worked! (i.e. verbally explaining things to you cat)
I recommend this book highly.

***** **Great for all Cat Owners!**
I love Pamela's approach to explaining how cats work. As she describes her own cats, I imagine my own little guy and how it perfectly lines up with how he is. I'd recommend this book to anyone who has a cat, loves cats, wants cats. I'd even go so far to say this is required reading for anyone who wants to start off on the right foot before adopting their own fur baby.
Thank you!

***** **Detailed and fun read - very informative**
What a detailed and refreshing approach. Because of this book I have further improved my understanding and relationships with my cats. Any cat lover would appreciate all the tips and tricks of this book and to anyone who doesn't quite "get" cats, or think they're vindictive creatures that don't how affection will be shown how to properly interpret cat behaviors and see the many signs of love cats give every day.

United Kingdom:

***** Don't understand cats, but want to get to know them better? Read this book. Got them and love them? Read this book.

For anyone who wants to know and understand their cats better - to really know how to deepen the relationship you have with cats and to enrich the environment for both you and your cat, this is the book to have. Pamela Merritt applies her experience, knowledge and tried and tested methods to show you how to achieve a closer relationship based on mutual respect, and understanding a cat's perspective of life. They are NOT dogs, so no use treating them like they are, or expecting them to behave like a dog. Pamela's approach is no everyday affair. It's warm, perceptive and it works.

If you enjoyed this book,
would you take a moment,
and leave a review on its Amazon page?

Thanks so much.
You have helped me help the kitties.

Made in the USA
San Bernardino, CA
03 August 2020

76396897R00166